AdvertisingAge

HANDBOOK of ADVERTISING

Herschell Gordon Lewis
Carol Nelson
Foreword by Rance Crain

NTC Business Books
NTC/Contemporary Publishing Group

Library of Congress Cataloging-in-Publication Data

Nelson, Carol, 1953–
    Advertising age handbook of advertising / Carol Nelson and Herschell
Gordon Lewis ; foreword by Rance Crain.
       p.   cm.
    Includes index.
    ISBN 0-8442-3670-5 (cloth)
    ISBN 0-8442-2448-0 (paper)
    1. Advertising—Handbooks, manuals, etc.   I. Lewis, Herschell Gordon,
1926– . II. Title.
HF5823.N36   1998
659.1—dc21   98-8362
                                                      CIP

Quotations from *Advertising Age* used with permission.

Cover design by Todd Petersen
Interior design by Impressions Book and Journal Services, Inc.

Published by NTC Business Books
A division of NTC/Contemporary Publishing Group, Inc.
4255 West Touhy Avenue, Lincolnwood (Chicago), Illinois 60646-1975 U.S.A.
Copyright © 1999 by NTC/Contemporary Publishing Group, Inc.
Printed in the United States of America
International Standard Book Number: 0-8442-3670-5 (cloth)
                                       0-8442-2448-0 (paper)

99 00 01 02 03 04 LB 19 18 17 16 15 14 13 12 11 10 9 8 7 6 5 4 3 2 1

Contents

Foreword

The advertising business has never been accused of being stagnant, but in the past decade or so, the pace of the business has markedly quickened as client, agency, and media consolidations have accelerated, media choices have expanded, and even the very nature of what constitutes advertising "creativity" has been called into question.

This is definitely not your father's ad business, and in today's advertising environment you can't tell the players (and the companies they work for) without a scorecard. Think of the *Advertising Age Handbook of Advertising* as your handy guide through the bumps and curves of the new advertising landscape.

Remember Philadelphia department store magnate John Wanamaker and his famous statement, "I know half my advertising budget is wasted. I just don't know which half"? In the one hundred years since old John uttered those immortal words, things have gotten worse.

When Mr. Wanamaker's emporium wanted to advertise its fine selection of merchandise to the Philadelphia populace, it had a few clear-cut choices: newspapers and circulars. It's hard to imagine that Wanamaker's could be wrong on its ad strategy 50 percent of the time with such limited media to select from, but maybe Mr. Wanamaker was referring not to media, but to choosing the right products to put in his ads. Should he play up the "softer side of Wanamaker's"?

So, if poor Mr. Wanamaker complained about his advertising batting average way back then, think how much more complicated the process is today. Not only do retail outlets have a lot more merchandise to promote, but they have a bewildering number of media choices with which to advertise their wares.

The *Advertising Age Handbook of Advertising* reflects this dilemma. If our handbook is coming out a little too late for Mr. Wanamaker, it can help you keep track of all the new media players—as well as budgeting, testing, research, and, of course, trying to figure out if your ad strategy is registering with consumers.

One of my favorite subjects explored in these pages is creative philosophy. It's always been my contention, to use an ad slogan from the old Benton & Bowles advertising agency, "It's not creative unless it sells," but there seems to be a rather strong contrary view developing. The latest theory is that ads shouldn't be so presumptuous as to sell the product directly and straightforwardly. Instead, advertising's new role is to show that your product shares the same values as your target market. As I recorded in my weekly *Advertising Age* column, which is reprinted on page 88, one ad guy told me his son likes those "Miller Time" beer ads because they're "weird," and presumably he likes the ads because he likes weird things.

One ad man, Ian Batey of the Batey Group in Singapore, made the point that media technology can also play havoc with creativity. "There's risk that technology can hijack creativity—will obscure the creative process. If you're creating a page in a newspaper or a page on the Internet, the fundamentals of brand-building still apply. You're still talking to human beings. You're still working with emotional art forms. You still have to tickle toes as well as heads."

Of course no single volume, such as this one, can possibly begin to tell an individual what he or she needs to know about the world of advertising, but I must say, it's not a bad starting place. Whether you're already in advertising or thinking of making this fascinating and dynamic field your career, I think you'll be glad to have our guide on your bookshelf.

Rance Crain
Editor in Chief
Advertising Age

Preface

Had a time traveler asked a group of advertising agency presidents in the year 1900, "What is your function?" the typical answer would have been, "To create and place advertising." Logical enough.

That same time traveler, revisiting an updated group of agency presidents (by now called CEOs or COOs) in the year 1950, would probably have elicited this answer: "To build brand image by advertising in selective media."

Comes the year 2000. The answer, if thoughtfully given, might be something like this: "As a marketing company, we partner in sales strategy and implement that strategy on a mass level."

Could further participation in the total marketing effort be the standard by the year 2050? This book will be well out of print by then, but the trends are clear: "Advertising" as a career has no future. The one-man gang is destined to handle accounts such as the local furniture store, but nothing more complex. The age of specialization has engulfed marketing as thoroughly as it has medicine. The classic opening questions, "Who are your customers, and what's your budget?" already are as obsolete as the one-man gang, even with half a century to the next time marker.

The dizzying array of media available to today's marketer poses two separate problems: First, media specialization is mandatory. Second, an understanding of the benefits and curses of each medium is mandatory.

This book proposes and explores the role of the advertising agency as total marketing partner. This is, if not the inevitable destiny of those in our profession, certainly the direction most likely to justify the word *professional*.

Planning has to extend far beyond a media schedule. Creative dare not isolate itself from salesmanship. Yet, with specialists assigned to each component, the complexity of structuring an effective advertising/marketing campaign is ever more challenging. Even more difficult is balancing short-range goals against long-range goals. The agency that explains an approach as having long-range effectiveness may well lose a client to an agency that can show the client quick results.

This book covers planning, of course, as well as budgeting, creative strategy, production, testing and research, and evaluation of what happens as the result of all this. In addition, we've included interviews with some current industry leaders who are candidly sharing their own opinions and philosophy.

All these are facets of the multiple interrelationships between agency and client as marketing partners. Some old-timers yearn for the kinder, gentler times in which the agency wrote and placed ads. But in an industry as dynamic as ours, there's no going back, nor should there be. The medical profession has gone far beyond leeches and mustard plaster as cures for ailments. Let us do likewise.

Herschell Gordon Lewis
Carol Nelson

Acknowledgments

We gleaned information from so many sources that naming them all might well require an auxiliary volume. Thanks are due not only to those with whom we talked but to those who over a great many years represented marketing wisdom that has become generic to the advertising profession.

Specifically, though, we must recognize the invaluable help given us by Cliff Einstein, Val Zammit, Michael Palmer, Stedman Graham, Chuck Peebler, Keith McCracken, Michael Drexler, and Tom Veazey—all of whose wisdom appears in these pages.

Encouragement and knowledge came from Margo Lewis, who for years has kept both us and our organization on track. We're grateful to Richard Hagle, who originated this project; Danielle Egan-Miller, our editor; and Heidi Bresnahan, our project editor; and Denise Betts, who has had the unenviable job of making sense out of hundreds of pages of text.

Most important of all: This book could not exist without the aid and cooperation of *Advertising Age,* whose huge weekly injection of information reflects the core of twenty-first-century marketing. And of course, to Rance Crain, the number-one statesman of our industry, our thanks for making this book possible.

We thank you all. We love you all.

▪ 1 ▪

The Purpose
of Advertising

Definition of terms is in order.

The mammoth and highly respected advertising agency Leo Burnett Co. has given the industry a logical interpretation of the word *advertising*. Actually, this definition tells us as much what advertising *isn't* as what it is: "It's *all* advertising"—that's what our marketing targets think. Whether it's television, newspaper, magazine, interactive, direct response, radio, sales promotion, or skywriting, it's all advertising.

Those people out there not only don't distinguish one medium from another, they're right to draw the conclusion they do. But if advertising is handled hyperprofessionally, the phrase *It's all advertising* becomes inconsequential.

What *is* consequential is which advertising produces a response other than recognition of the message as advertising.

Identifying with the Customer

"Don't think like the seller. Think like the sellee."

One reason so much of the television advertising in the late 1990s resulted in high "noted" ratings and flat sales was attention to

1

technique rather than salesmanship. Some commercials costing $1 million or more, plus an eight-figure media budget, never did have any impact on the advertiser's bottom line.

Of course, this could be because the product itself was not something the target audience would want—a sign of defective market research. But the cause also could stem from a defective marketing philosophy: Getting attention = effectiveness.

The partnership between an advertiser and its agency becomes fragile either when the agency accepts a prefabricated approach in which the agency has no confidence or when the execution of a concept by the agency places form over substance.

In Chapter 7 we identify the difference between research and testing. Both, obviously, are imperfect gauges of human behavior, if only because the typical human being cannot decode perfectly his or her own motivations. But research should prevent a straying from the solid rails leading from the depot (read: Item for Sale) to the destination (read: Ignition of Desire to Buy).

Years ago, when the Detroit advertising agency Campbell-Ewald handled Chevrolet advertising, its key executives had to make an annual pilgrimage to a Chevrolet dealership. There, under battle conditions, they had firsthand connection with prospective Chevrolet buyers. This forced the agency viewpoint to be congruent with buyer attitudes.

Today we have, especially for packaged goods, bar codes which become "tellers" at the point of ultimate decision—the checkout counter. Twenty-first-century reading of bar codes tells us quickly how effective our most recent commercials have been. To a somewhat lesser extent, coupon redemption (also bar-coded) tells us whether under any circumstances our marketing or our product can crack the barrier of habit.

Customers today cannot be identified with a single noun. Suppose we take the word *seniors*. Is this a coherent, homogenized group? Even into the 1990s, many advertisers regarded seniors as seniors. Now our databases identify at least three separate categories of seniors—and for major campaigns, perhaps half a dozen more.

For example, we have seniors on a fixed income. These individuals buy cautiously because they must. We have seniors who are still in the workforce. These individuals fight to maintain equivalence with their juniors and will spend money to do so. We have seniors who have amassed sufficient estate to live at least as comfortably as they did when they were in the workforce and now have the additional bonus of ample leisure time. These individuals seek to maximize the availability of leisure time and their own physical ability to enjoy it.

Are all three groups parallel? Certainly they are. They all are seniors. They all share, attitudinally, the senior position of having earned an "edge." Are all three groups parallel for the purposes of selling to a specific advertiser? Certainly they are not. Some are useless targets for a pitch that lumps all seniors together; some may require tailored messages catering to—but not transparently so—their own category within the category; some may be the only group within the giant senior market who *can* respond.

So, for contemporary advertising to justify every cent of expense—and that is exactly what contemporary advertising has to do if the agency wants to keep the account and the company advertising department wants to keep their jobs—the message has to identify with the customer. More! It has to do so without being recognized as boilerplate advertising. This is the core of professionalism the advertising world has every right to expect from its members in the twenty-first century.

On a business-to-business level, identifying with the customer presents a paradox. It is both easier and more difficult than a parallel circumstance approaching consumers. Easier: Advertisers know immediately who their targets are and, equally valuable, what the competitive marketing circumstances are. More difficult: Advertisers have to be aware of the competitive marketplace, in which their targets can quickly penetrate claims that represent "advertising" instead of recognizable benefit.

Turning loose a creative team unschooled in the mechanics of what is being offered for sale is an equivalent paradox. The negative is that this team can stumble into mistakes that look stupid to the advertiser's corporate executives. The positive is that, in the absence of being steeped in corporate lore, this team may well be better able to sell benefit (what it will do for me) instead of product (what it is).

In a sense, the previous paragraph may be a microcosm of justification for an advertising agency's existence in the marketing mix. Smart advertising doesn't regurgitate the structure of what is being sold. Smart advertising presents that magical word *benefit*.

Communicating with the Customer

Note the common denominator for these statements:

- "Nobody reads direct mail."
- "Nobody pays any attention to television commercials."
- "The Internet is a huge advertising graveyard."
- "Only retailers can sell in the newspapers."
- "Radio has no mnemonic value."
- "Magazines sit unread for weeks at a time."

What do these statements have in common? Surprisingly, they all can be true. But that doesn't mean they *are* true.

The tightrope an advertiser walks is encapsulated in these statements. If we don't get our target's attention, no message has been transmitted. If, on the other hand, all we do is get attention, we have violated basic rules of salesmanship.

This is why we have every right to call advertising a profession and not a craft or trade. The professional advertising expert is a true communicator. He or she knows which medium reaches the proper targets. Even more consequentially, he or she knows how to break through the crust of indifference, apathy, or even hostility that lies between the message sender and the message recipient.

Is the medium the message? Certainly, so far as that incomplete statement goes. Without the proper medium to carry it, the message is wasted—a tree falling in the forest with no one to hear it.

Now let's complete the equation. Within the proper medium, a message that is noncompetitive with other messages has too weak an impact to generate a response. So the relationship between medium and message gains importance as we begin to analyze optimal means of communicating with the customer.

Add to this the "X" factor: experimentation.

Example: Every competitor is advertising in the media the entire industry accepts as proper media for what is being advertised. One aggressive marketer goes boldly forth where no one has gone before. Three possibilities exist:

1. The advertising will bomb because it simply is not reaching the proper targets.
2. The advertising will succeed on a level acceptably parallel to advertising in traditional media.
3. The advertising will be a bonanza because it taps a vein of gold not previously discovered.

Obviously, it is the search for this last El Dorado that impels some brave agencies (and clients) to experiment. Obviously, too, it is the fear of failure that keeps some agencies (and clients) on the well-trodden trails.

Each attitude has solid logic behind it. The agency's charge is to use its client dollars most effectively in communicating with customers-to-be. Who can quarrel with the interpretation that this means discovering what has worked in the past and using this as the litmus test for what will work in the future? But if this were the only argument that could be mounted, a handful of media would be loaded with identical advertising by identically competing advertisers. The answer to customer communication isn't necessarily a blend of the traditional and the experimental. This is a gray area to be explored on a case-by-case basis as the market for a product or service matures and reaches saturation within any target group.

Increasing Desire, Increasing Sales

A couple of generations ago, the 3M Company recognized a dangerous fact: The use of Scotch tape to repair torn paper had reached saturation. For the company's output of this product to increase, new uses had to be found.

And they were. 3M advertising consistently suggested new uses, and new uses recruited new users.

Arm & Hammer also devoted much of its marketing muscle, as well as its research facilities, to exploiting new uses for its baking soda.*

More recently, companies such as Intel and Microsoft *forced* market acceptance by forcing obsolescence.

Had any of these companies rested on its laurels, as such products as Alka-Seltzer and Anacin did in the 1980s, their market share would have plummeted. For those products, market share in the 1990s was a fraction of what it was in the 1970s.

Another example is Coca-Cola. Old-timers remember when Coca-Cola was available in six-ounce bottles, and *only* in six-ounce bottles. Pepsi-Cola tried to break the Coca-Cola stranglehold with one of the earliest memorable jingles:

> *Pepsi-Cola hits the spot.*
> *Twelve full ounces, that's a lot.*
> *Twice as much for a nickel too.*
> *Pepsi-Cola is the drink for you.*

Pepsi's *raison d'être,* in its entirety, was a comparative: Pepsi-Cola offered twice as much cola. Yes, the taste was not identical, but the average person—despite the advertising claims each cola drink makes—did not regard this as a key determinant. Pepsi positioned itself and was able to claim part of the cola market.

Today both Pepsi and Coke are available in a dizzying variety of brand extensions. Each brand extension has its own advertising budget and its own image. The advertising for the diet version of either drink has little relationship with the advertising for the original brand. The original brand itself is on U.S. supermarket shelves primarily in twelve-ounce cans and two-liter bottles. What we don't see is the original packaging. (Rumors surface almost every year about Coke restoring the six-ounce bottle, which still is available in some countries.)

Advertising hasn't changed either product at all. What advertising *has* done has been to change the competitive ambience in which the battle has been joined on a multilevel basis.

When advertising attempts to change the image of product, results can go either way but always at the mercy of the merciless consumer. Witness "New Coke," one of the great marketing disasters of the late twentieth century.

What the formulators, backed up by the marketing team, ignored was the fact any consumer might have told them: There are Coke drinkers, and there are Pepsi drinkers, and the reason Coke drinkers prefer Coke is because the taste of Coke is what they are used to.

Advertising can lead to exposure, but advertising can lead to acceptance only when the projection of image overrides basic tastes. You can lead a consumer to New Coke, but you can't make him or her drink more than once. So big a failure was this campaign that word leaked—some say from Coca-Cola headquarters that the substitution of New Coke and subsequent triumphant reintroduction of "Classic Coke"—the original product with an updated name—was deliberate.

Should we blame an advertising department or an advertising agency for product failure? The answer is as muddy as the question, because we have situations such as the Edsel automobile, in which the product demonstrated no uniqueness, nor did its advertising. We have situations such as wine coolers, which burst upon public consciousness with advertising that sometimes was brilliant, quickly became a passing fad, and could not be rescued regardless of the number of dollars poured into its promotion.

Only the most naive naysayer or the most disgruntled ex-employee can ever claim that advertising has no impact on increasing desire. Many years ago Procter & Gamble concluded that everyone knew the advantages of Ivory soap. The advertising budget was slashed; sales plummeted. Until shortly after World War II, the Hershey Company's advertising budget was zero. The company felt the quality of its product alone was ample incentive to buy. Today Hershey is a major advertiser—and has to be, to compete in the twenty-first-century marketplace.

With the product code on almost every item sold through retail outlets, it now becomes both practical and logical to gauge the effect advertising has on packaged goods such as those sold in supermarkets. Advertising is, of course, the sole rationale behind success or failure of a product sold directly. Which leads us to the next section of this chapter.

Integrated Marketing

One of the more pleasant developments of the period from 1985 onward has been the disappearance of the competitive nature separating the various disciplines of advertising and marketing. One doesn't have to be an old-timer to remember the get-off-my-turf attitude and mutual suspicions and backbiting that attended a full-court press in which a marketer decided to employ media advertising, direct marketing, public relations, and sales promotions such as point-of-purchase.

What forced the hand of advertising agencies was less a burst of statesmanship than the realization that they were losing partial or total control over marketing campaigns. The result was consolidation and merger between advertising agencies and companies specializing in other aspects of marketing. The happy result, for all concerned— marketer as well as agency—has been seamless integration of the various disciplines without animosity or jealousy or artificial denigration of a useful avenue. In the twenty-first century the term *advertising agency* may well be replaced by a more apt and more effective term, *marketing agency.*

To those who give lip service to integrated marketing but fail to understand how each component adds a separate dimension, adding a toll-free number to a conventional television commercial equals integration: "After all, we're selling brand, and we're also providing a response mechanism." Oddly, to an extent their conclusion is valid, but what is missing is an evaluation of the comparative media that might be called to action with greater results per dollar spent.

The Internet has added yet another dimension—and another source of confusion. Exposure on the Internet, in the medium's early years, seems to be an end rather than a means. Separate departments set up at agencies and their clients operate in what might be regarded as a different universe. Who is the target of Internet advertising? Only now are marketers separating the medium from the message.

Banners and links, for many Internet marketers, appear in places unrelated to sites logical buyers might be visiting. Speculative targeting is a venerable marketing technique; its effectiveness invariably is linked to coincidental marketing aimed at primary prospects.

Does Loyalty Still Exist?

Does agency/client loyalty exist—*on either side*? Or is the whole notion of loyalty obsolete, in a cold-blooded era in which each party has little regard for the other's security?

It's no novelty for apparent loyalties to dissolve like tissue in boiling water. We see evidence everywhere: A "freebie" at a fast-food restaurant shatters whatever fragile loyalty a diner may have had to a competitor. So why should anyone be surprised when a new executive takes over and the agency, whose efforts contributed greatly to the client's success, is summarily replaced . . . or when an agency pitches a new client and arbitrarily resigns a "loyal" account?

Cynical and heartless? It depends on your position in the struggle. If advertising couldn't influence the buying decision, what would be the point of having, as advisors, advertising experts . . . or this book?

2

Planning the Communication

What is an advertising message supposed to accomplish?

A surprising number of advertiser/marketers make this the last decision when planning a campaign. Success depends largely on its being the first decision, however, because the answer to that question is the key determinant for the other two facets of marketing planning—media and budget.

Defining Objectives

In kinder, gentler times, marketers recognized three "phases" of product promotion: introductory, competitive, and retentive. Today's budgets make such a philosophy a luxury in which many marketers can't afford to indulge.

The result is that many of today's marketing programs leap directly into the competitive phase and never do enjoy the placid waters of the retentive phase.

The retentive aspect has evolved into a different twenty-first-century direction—relationship marketing. Relationship marketing is not universally accepted, nor is it universally advisable, nor practical.

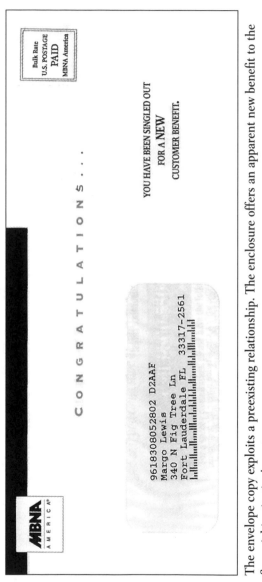

The envelope copy exploits a preexisting relationship. The enclosure offers an apparent new benefit to the financial institution's customer.

Obviously, it cannot be applied to the introduction of a product where no relationship or image preexists. So the objective of today's start-up has to be dynamic, unsubtle, and totally targeted. The difficulty of total targeting lies in the inability to draw a perfect conclusion of who the target should be. Such a conclusion, to be valid, can just as readily stem from marketing results as it can from marketing projections.

An example of well-planned targeting was Chrysler's introduction of the Plymouth Neon. The first exposure of this car was during a Super Bowl football broadcast—reaching a predetermined target group. In fact, the single word *Hi* perfectly matched the casual image of its targets. The success of this car has depended on purchases by a fairly narrow demographic segment.

Another automobile, Saturn, had an entirely different objective: establishing itself outside the orbit of other General Motors cars, with a product that was not dramatically different from other cars. The theme, "A different kind of company, a different kind of car," plus monies devoted to rewards for buyer loyalty, resulted in owners who were Saturn disciples and who attended reunions at the company's headquarters in Tennessee.

After six years of this campaign, the objectives changed to expand beyond buyers who could be attracted solely by the product introduction, which was wearing thin. In Saturn's case, objectives followed the traditional path: first, introductory; then, competitive.

IBM, whose reputation for conservatism in marketing might be well deserved, occasionally institutes loyalty programs for its stockholders. One such program offered a discount on a personal computer. As is proper with such an offer, the opportunity had a specific and firm expiration date. The concept of rewarding stockholders, while certainly not new, serves a double purpose because it builds loyalty on two levels: ownership of the stock and ownership of the product.

Long-Range Versus Short-Range Planning

Even the most statesmanlike marketer finds it difficult to consider long-range planning instead of short-range planning. Long-range planning has two perils: First, one must anticipate what the competition will do. Second, one has to guess at the socioeconomic circumstances far outside any area in which the marketer can exert immediate or long-range influence.

The need for a vision of where you want to be increases in difficulty as you plan—or guess—the temporal distance to destination, economically and in terms of market share. Actually, difficulty increases geometrically from weekly to monthly to annually to any goal beyond one year (which qualifies as "long range").

Obviously, anyone can write a "plan" based on a predetermined formula. Such plans, neatly bound and distributed within an organization, seem to acquire a cachet because they represent organized thought. But in today's fast-changing marketing environment, a plan made at 10:00 A.M. may be obsolete at 4:00 P.M. So the key to long-term planning is constant reassessment of ongoing short-term plans.

Most progressive organizations know where they want to be in one to five years. But they don't memorialize their intention in a document they then file in a drawer; they incorporate their goal into their day-to-day operations, adjusting as they go.

Not All Plans Are the Same (Nor Should They Be)

A surprising number of marketing organizations base their marketing plans on what the competition is doing. This isn't a good idea. The notion that two competing companies are parallel is as invalid as the notion that two side-by-side homes are parallel. Yes, they are in the same neighborhood; no, they are not interchangeable. So the marketer who says, "My product is different," refutes his or her own argument by basing a plan on that of a competitor.

Marketing Plan Objectives

What objectives, then, should enter into a marketing plan of any length, whether for the week or for the decade? Some of the components should include those from the list on page 17:

In the same issue of a national newspaper, two hotels ran competing ads. But do they compete? Each positions itself to attract a specific demographic group. The Westin ad (on the next page) is family-oriented in both graphics and text. The Ritz-Carlton ad (above) is totally upscale. The fine print in the Ritz-Carlton ad contains the sentence "To take advantage of these special summer rates, you must charge your stay with your American Express Card." The phrase *you must* would be totally out of key in the happy-go-lucky Westin ad.

- Realistic and attainable sales goals
- Realistic analysis of the present marketplace
- Realistic analysis of the potential marketplace
- Dispassionate analysis of competitors' strengths and weaknesses
- Number of dollars necessary to achieve marketing goals
- Flexibility and adaptability among the entire administrative, marketing, and financial departments
- Realistic timelines
- Multiple allowances for contingencies

Elements of the Typical Advertising Plan

Only the most naive marketer or advertising agency regards budget as the be-all and end-all of advertising planning. Only slightly less naive is the marketer or advertising agency who subdivides a budget into various media and regards the result as a "marketing plan."

Naivete tends to disappear when we add additional logical components to the planning mixture. Research may or may not give us totally accurate predictions of how well what we are selling *should* perform in the competitive marketplace, but certainly any such information should be folded into the marketing plan.

Contingencies have to include such elements as these:

- Rebates if necessary (if the market softens)
- Changes in regional, national, and international distribution
- Updating, upgrading, and changes in whatever we are selling
- Possible changes in types of customers and in ways a product is used
- Changes in media, such as happened when the Internet became a viable marketing tool
- Constant reinterpretation of the database
- Expansion or contraction of target markets
- Unexpected success for which production capability is not immediately available
- Introduction of legal restrictions or governmental actions

Formation of the marketing plan, then, should not be an automatic chore. Rather, it should be a "live" document kept on the table for constant action and reevaluation.

Caution!

In a database-driven organization, salesmanship can slowly give way to the recitation of fact. The salesperson knows that positive results come from *selective* facts rather than totality, because totality invariably includes elements that damage both image and effectiveness.

The most valid caution is to avoid compiling but not using data. An annoying trend seems to be "database for the sake of database." If data are not useful, both money and time are better spent in other directions . . . but . . . data are useful.

Relationship Marketing as an Objective-Definer

One-on-one marketing used to be left to the dealer. The manufacturer and/or distributor felt that the corporate role was to develop a generic motivation; the dealer's role was to refine the motivation on an individual level among those who responded to mass marketing.

One of the fastest-growing areas of advertising—and the change is almost sudden—is the devotion of primary advertising dollars to relationship marketing. This isn't entirely because of a recognition of the value of one-on-one; it's just as much due to improvement in access to data—who is buying what, who isn't buying what, who should be buying what, and why the various "who" individuals are or are not responding to specific messages.

Two automotive marketers have established ongoing relationship marketing programs to maintain buyer loyalty and to add cachet to the concept of ownership. Jeep, in 1995, initiated Camp Jeep, which included an off-road trek using Jeep's four-wheel drive, instruction in four-wheel driving, bright entertainment, and conversations with

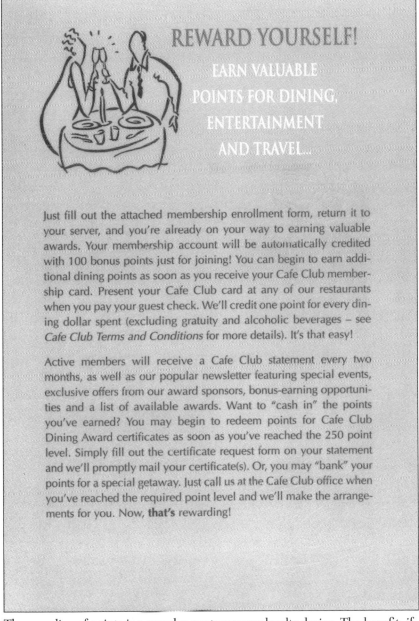

REWARD YOURSELF!

EARN VALUABLE POINTS FOR DINING, ENTERTAINMENT AND TRAVEL...

Just fill out the attached membership enrollment form, return it to your server, and you're already on your way to earning valuable awards. Your membership account will be automatically credited with 100 bonus points just for joining! You can begin to earn additional dining points as soon as you receive your Cafe Club membership card. Present your Cafe Club card at any of our restaurants when you pay your guest check. We'll credit one point for every dining dollar spent (excluding gratuity and alcoholic beverages – see *Cafe Club Terms and Conditions* for more details). It's that easy!

Active members will receive a Cafe Club statement every two months, as well as our popular newsletter featuring special events, exclusive offers from our award sponsors, bonus-earning opportunities and a list of available awards. Want to "cash in" the points you've earned? You may begin to redeem points for Cafe Club Dining Award certificates as soon as you've reached the 250 point level. Simply fill out the certificate request form on your statement and we'll promptly mail your certificate(s). Or, you may "bank" your points for a special getaway. Just call us at the Cafe Club office when you've reached the required point level and we'll make the arrangements for you. Now, **that's** rewarding!

The awarding of points is a popular contemporary loyalty device. The benefit, if the points have quick value and, in greater numbers, have strong value, is that the customer is held in the program. Points closely parallel airline frequent flyer programs.

some of the company's technicians. Jeep's direct marketing executive made this comment: "The events are opportunities to meet the corporation one-on-one." He pointed out that many Jeep owners who attended the event expressed great surprise that the parent company would underwrite this kind of one-to-one public relations.

Jeep's activity parallels a relationship marketing program by Land Rover. Owners of Range Rovers, the top-of-the-line Land Rover, receive invitations to off-road activities.

Mercedes-Benz of North America also involved itself in a relationship marketing program by sending new owners a camera. The technique was to ask the owners to take photographs of their car and the way it became part of their lifestyle. The automobile company then developed the film at no cost to the owner and used some of the photos in its relationship marketing program.

While this was happening, Cadillac—an upscale General Motors car—invaded the lower echelons with a new model called the Catera. Introductory advertising for this model, confusing to some, was "the Caddy that zigs." Catera advertising obviously did not aim itself at the traditional Cadillac buyer, who represented a considerably older demographic group. In attempting to bring younger buyers into the fold, any brand risks alienating its traditional buyers/supporters—a dangerous ploy, but sometimes necessary, as the buyer base either ages or shrinks.

Demography Dictates Change

A reverse example of switching based on awareness of demographic changes: the original on-line services promotions, which, logically enough, aim themselves at Generation X. This group was targeted through media discreetly aimed at them; others were largely ignored—until a researcher discovered that one of the fastest-growing groups of on-line users was people aged fifty-five and older. By the time this discovery resulted in diversion of marketing dollars to intensify participation in on-line services, this target group already was increasing based on word of mouth. The spillover then resulted in dramatically increased attention within the World Wide Web.

Appeals to Generation X—the under-35s—can take a position that might irritate and annoy older consumers. This ad typifies in-your-face advertising: "It's better—it's smarter—it's cheaper. So why are you still sitting there?"

Long Term Versus Short Term

Long-range planning is out of fashion. Technology has outstripped the ability to predict what will happen in a competitive marketplace.

Most marketers in 1994 would have been nonplussed by the suggestion that part of the advertising budget be allocated to the Internet. "The Internet? What's that?" Within a single year, every major advertiser had a Web site.

The fallout was subtle but definitely there. Television advertisers, aiming the bulk of their messages at an age group skewed toward the under-forties, suddenly saw mass defections. These people led the way to the Internet during the hours in which they had previously watched situation comedies on television.

It is a given that an advertiser has to migrate with its targets. Asking the *targets* to perform the migration, in the twenty-first century, is an arrogant futility.

Long-term planning also has another implicit time bomb: product life. In packaged goods, loyalties swing wildly, and trends can disappear even before many consumer segments are aware of them.

Developing Market Strategy

Strategy and budget (budget being the topic of the next chapter) are the scrambled eggs of marketing—two components that, once assembled, cannot logically be separated from each other. This is because budget is not (at least, it should not be) a stand-alone element.

The advertising agency that asks its client or prospective client, "What's your budget?" is asking a logical question only if that question follows an intense discussion of what a campaign is supposed to accomplish. Even then, the logic of the question can be blunted by similar questions asked of competing companies by *their* advertising agencies. Asking the question before receiving an indication of what is to be accomplished is both arrogant and amateurish, and it is totally out of fashion in a database-driven competitive ambience of the twenty-first century.

Because products and trends both are cyclical, an analysis of the marketing climate can tell the marketer to some extent whether or not the strategy has to include an educational aspect. In the world of fashion, skirt length and tie width aren't major elements because the fashion-conscious targets anticipate annual or semiannual change. A more dramatic, more dynamic marketing ploy, such as a direct attack on the category leader, requires considerable research and equally considerable speculation on what the prospective buyers will or won't accept. Too, as vendors have discovered for thousands of years, enthusiasm or lack of it for total economic conditions can skew demand, generate it, or kill it.

An example is the effect of the gasoline crunch of 1973. Suddenly, smaller cars reached unexpected heights of popularity. The image of the small-car owner, similarly, underwent a quick change from someone who couldn't afford a big car to someone who was an astute (and even patriotic) buyer. This episode indicates the value of the correlation between a public relations effort to create an image and an advertising effort to cash in on that image.

In the late 1990s, by which time the attitude toward high gasoline prices had stabilized, big cars once again became popular. The market, then, showed a reaction to forces that were oblique to original consumer demand. For that matter, advertising for gasoline brands exploded from a period of near quiescence. The twenty-first century undoubtedly will see a different kind of competitive advertising between gasoline brands and electric cars. Thus, the marketing climate doesn't always depend on a directly competitive marketplace but is just as sensitive to elements determining what products are politically and economically correct.

Having analyzed the marketing climate, advertisers face a second decision: the extent to which they have the desire or the financial capability to achieve dominance within that climate. Products, such as Snapple, the soft drink Quaker acquired and for which it had such strong marketing hopes, were unable to achieve not only dominance but also parity because the advertising couldn't project a clear image.

Determining Proper Prospects and Targets

At the time of the industrial revolution, a marketer recognized three "wants"—food, clothing, and shelter. As the economic circumstances of more people improved, those wants kept pace by sophisticating themselves—tasty food, fashionable clothing, and superior shelter. As the workweek shrank from sixty hours to forty-eight hours to forty hours to (in many cases today) twenty-five hours, the number of proper prospects and targets for leisure items has expanded to keep pace. And so has the variety of products designed to take advantage of a greater percentage of potential buyers.

(Obviously, an increase in population also plays a role in establishing the total number of individuals whose circumstances—social as well as economic—warrant inclusion in a prospect/target group.)

Where professional marketing becomes paramount over mass advertising is in an ability to recognize "speculative" targets and uses. The 3M Company vastly expanded its market for adhesive tapes by expanding public awareness of uses beyond repairing torn sheets of paper. Similarly, Arm & Hammer developed whole new echelons of users beyond those who used baking soda in baking. In fact, so many individuals were using baking soda as a dentifrice that the company, quite logically, successfully launched a dentifrice. Other consumers, led by the company's awareness campaigns, were using baking soda in their washing machines as a deodorizer; the logical next product: Arm & Hammer deodorizing laundry detergent.

No amount of advertising and no strategy, however brilliant, can overcome obsolescence caused by improved competitive products. Just as, in the 1930s, toothpaste made tooth powder obsolete, so have some of the bestselling toothpastes become obsolete as new formulations appear. Consider Pepsodent, the bellwether Unique Selling Proposition product of Ted Bates in its Rosser Reeves heyday, whose slogan is still included in classic advertising anthologies: "You'll wonder where the yellow went when you brush your teeth with Pepsodent." It and Ipana have vanished into history, just as some of the bestselling toothpastes of the 1990s already are showing age and giving way to more contemporary tooth-whitening compounds. Fluoride, at one time the magical word for selling toothpaste, is no longer a viable hook on which to hang the hope of sale. No uniqueness remains.

Generations ago *The Saturday Evening Post* pointed out that when a publication artificially expands its circulation base by either lowering its rates or circularizing on a mass level, the buying power of the typical resulting subscriber will drop—which changes the optimal type of advertising within that publication. Awareness of this no longer drives media the way it once did, but reaching proper targets is still a matter of medium as well as message. This is one reason for the surge of interest in direct marketing with its pinpointing capabilities.

The concept that "our proper target is anyone who is willing to buy what we have to sell" can be damaging. Witness the furor in the late 1990s over Joe Camel, an icon of hipness whose reach extended too far.

Users, New Users, and Switched Customers

A newspaper, in a campaign to attract advertisers to its neighborhood sections, divided prospects into three groups: "Lost Sheep" (prior advertisers who no longer placed advertising in the paper), "Newcomers" (companies that had never advertised in this newspaper before), and "Live Wires" (existing advertisers). Although the end intention was identical—expanded advertising within the pages of this section—the approach to each of these groups necessarily differed. To the Lost Sheep, the sales argument had to combine the themes of lost revenues on the part of the advertiser and improved readership. To the Newcomers, the approach was the necessity of being in the newspaper's pages in order to achieve any kind of expanded community awareness and immediate revenue increases. To Live Wires, either of the two previous approaches would have been senseless, so the targeted communication to this group centered around an offer of lowered rates for an expanded schedule.

Nothing was surprisingly inventive about this campaign. It typified the need for segmenting customers into groups, not only recognizable on the seller level, but also recognizable by the buyers themselves.

Earlier in this book, we pointed out that the days of product introduction as a separate phase of marketing are almost gone. To attract a new user, whether on a consumer level or on a business level, an advertiser has to leap immediately into the roiling competitive waters, finding a real or at least ostensible product benefit.

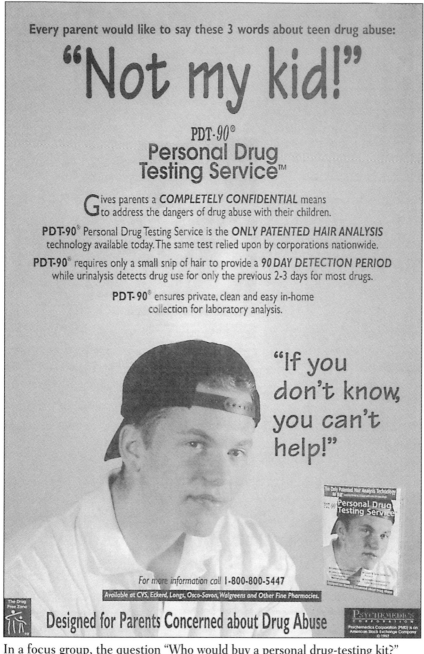

In a focus group, the question "Who would buy a personal drug-testing kit?" might elicit dozens of answers. This marketer aggressively positions the kit, aiming it at parents of teenagers. To underscore the positioning, the product itself has a photograph—not illustrative art—of a "typical" teenager. A competitor might counterposition a product simply by having a bland, all-type product name on the box. Visualize the point of sale: Is the photo a positive or negative force when an individual decides whether to buy this product?

That benefit may not be the same for new users as it is for those whom the marketer wants to recruit from the ranks of users of competitive products. The problem, obviously, is that an advertising message can target only one group at a time if the advertising is to have any power. Part of the solution is using targeted media. Nordic Track, for example, matched its message to the readership of individual publications aimed at age, interest, and gender groups.

Cruise lines represent classic examples of attracting new users, switched customers, and intensified activity among existing customers. In this highly competitive business, the successful cruise lines position themselves to represent status within a specific demographic/sociological posture. One cruise line may project the image of sedateness and style, so a young couple implicitly knows that cruise is not for them. Another cruise line projects a glittering "Las Vegas" image. A retired couple may well respond to this, knowing they are atypical of the apparent personality profile, in order to assure themselves that they have not succumbed to the very sedateness and style that typify the other cruise line's clientele.

Positioning: Establishing the Marketplace Niche

Image and offer—which, really, equate to positioning—dictate the creative strategy by which a campaign takes form. Chapter 4 explores techniques for linking positioning and creative strategy.

The term *Unique Selling Proposition* (usp) was coined by the latter-day pioneer Rosser Reeves (chairman of the Ted Bates agency in its salad days and author of *Reality in Advertising*, a 1961 book that is still worthwhile reading in which Reeves deals a well-deserved blow to his confreres who venerated message over sales). Some of Reeves's campaigns are still remembered more than a third of a century later: "You'll wonder where the yellow went when you brush your teeth with Pepsodent"; the "megatane" rating for gasoline; the hammer-in-the-head campaign for Anacin.

NEVER OVERSHADOWED.
AT 25.9 LBS. AND $799! IT'S
EVEN EASIER TO CLIMB ON A KLEIN.
FOR THE KLEIN DEALER NEAREST YOU,
CALL 1-800-52-KLEIN.

KLEIN

From children testing their first two-wheelers to retirement community "biker gangs" who ride to the mall and back every day, almost everybody rides a bicycle. To whom does a bicycle ad appeal? Consider the ad above and those on the next three pages. The Klein ad strives for a universal marketplace; its terminology is neutral. The Giant ad is aimed at the independent-minded young woman. The Schwinn ad combines humor with the type of artificial smugness some like to assume toward celebrities. The San Andreas ad is a statement of assumed superiority, obviously aimed at the upscale bicycle aficionado.

⚡GIANT.

LEGENDARY FEMALE TOLERANCE OF BULLET-
CHOMPING PAIN IS NO EXCUSE FOR RIDING A
MAN'S BIKE. THE UNNEUTERED ATX 875™ IS A HIGH
PERFORMANCE DESIGN OF CU92™ ALUMINUM,
BUILT FOR A WOMAN'S DECIDEDLY DIFFERENT
PHYSIQUE. ITS SPECIAL GEOMETRY AFFORDS A
PREVIOUSLY UNHEARD OF COMFORT WITH
WHICH TO BLAZE TRAILS, CRUSH OPPONENTS AND
BURY MISCONCEPTIONS FROM HERE TO VIENNA.

LISTEN UP FREUD, WE DON'T EVEN ENVY THEIR BIKES ANYMORE.

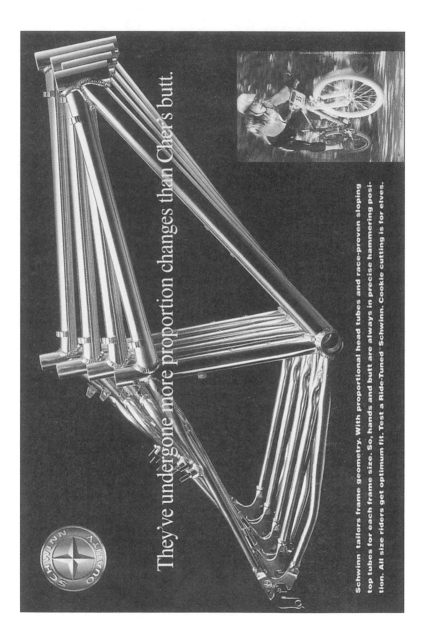

They've undergone more proportion changes than Cher's butt.

To understand the concept of positioning and the USP, analyze the wording of the Pepsodent message. It doesn't say that *only* Pepsodent gets the yellow out. It positions Pepsodent so that no competitor can make the identical claim.

Writing in the pages of *Advertising Age*, Editor-in-Chief Rance Crain observed in mid-1997:

> *Rosser Reeves' book made a lot of sense (maybe because he was the brother-in-law of David Ogilvy, who said he was ordering 450 copies—"one for each member of my staff and one for every client").*

> *Readers are adjured to "think of* USP *not so much as something you put into an advertisement. Think of* USP *as something the consumer takes out of an advertisement."*

Crain points out that *Advertising Age* itself had warned the advertising community against "hopping on the USP bandwagon." The rationale: "If all the agencies in America were to flock to the USP standard, we'd need fast—fast—FAST relief. The air would be hideous with the echoing claim and the diagrammatic complaint, and the poor audience would be cowering before the most tasteless and strident barrage of commercials in history."

As powerful as it was in the mid-twentieth century, is the USP concept still valid today? Also writing in *Advertising Age,* Michael Bungey, then chairman-CEO of Bates Worldwide, pointed out that this concept

> *was and still is the most robust foundation yet devised for raising the probability of producing persuasive, competitive, effective advertising. In today's volatile marketplace it is more relevant than ever because the* USP *is a consumer-driven, marketing-led approach that jibes with clients' needs and consumers' desires.* USP *advertising is about creating a consumer response—not just transmitting information.*

Thus, industry spokespeople agree, the value of this concept is timeless because it is tied directly to salesmanship, not to a murky creative plan driven by awareness rather than marketing.

Two Factors for Positioning

Two factors enter into the consideration for positioning a product or service. The first is *demography*—the selection of the "who." Who represents the logical responder to your message? The "who" factor dictates media selection, and this choice represents the most amount of money dedicated to any campaign. Sometimes, in product introduction, demography results from imperfect media research. The result is, with luck, discovery of a vastly expanded marketplace. The result is, without luck, a failed campaign in which too often the advertiser concludes that the market is not ready for this product.

The second factor is *competitive*—giving the prospective customer or client a comparative reason for preference. Even if media selection is perfect, the wrong decision in product positioning within the chosen demographic group or groups will result in an ineffective marketing program.

So the first factor, demography, is an intellectualized decision that may result from research, prior marketing experience, or an empirical point of view (which, strangely, is often just as accurate as research and prior marketing experience). The second factor, competitive, is largely a creative process based on sound principles of marketing. Where the creative process sometimes may mislead the campaign's direction is in an assumption that members of a demographic group want to be addressed *as* members of that group.

A theory of marketing (that has great validity) is that marketers can't make a mistake by overflattering their targets. For major marketers (as the discontinued Cadillac Cimarron exemplified), an appeal aimed at a lower demographic segment, leaning on an established position, can damage the original image even while establishing the second. This may explain why so many major brands are supercautious about brand extensions and often will introduce a new product using the established name only as a touchstone, not as another line within that brand name.

In the hyperspecialized marketing ambience of the twenty-first century, positioning becomes even more important than it has been in previous times. A marketer will appoint a separate advertising agency to establish a position with a specific ethnic or racial group, gender, or perceived time-in-life niche.

Validating Desire: Exorcising the Specter of Buyer Remorse

A venerable concept of almost any kind of salesmanship is that a product is what it is plus what the buyer thinks it is. Often, in a retail store, the salesperson will effect the sale of a suit based on brand name rather than on fit. The buyer preens because of an imagined benefit—which, actually, is not imagined: owning a suit with that label somehow seems to make it a better fit.

Direct-marketing practitioners have known for at least two centuries that adding a congratulatory message with merchandise shipped improves the "stick rate"—that is, the percentage retained and not returned for credit.

Those who disparage image advertising overlook its ultimate value at the point of sale. Those who embrace and endorse integrated advertising recognize or sense the motivators underlying a buyer's acceptance of what he or she has bought—either grudging, accepting, or advocating.

The mixture is not always exquisite in its percentages of establishing a favorable climate and convincing the ultimate target to enjoy that climate. Advertising is, after all, still an inexact science. In fact, many who control its destiny and reputation regard it as an art form, not a science at all.

But it certainly has been proved, tens of thousands of times, that a consumer or a business enterprise will pay more for a product or service that has achieved a reputation in the marketplace than for a generic. The shelves of retail stores and the bottles in druggists' supply cabinets often prove that a generic product or a house brand may be identical in composition, effectiveness, flavor, and stability to its better-known competitor. But not only can a generic never demand the same price a well-known product can demand—after all, price is the principal reason generics exist at all—but the proof of the value of brand name in combating buyer remorse is the preponderance of buyers who, even realizing that two products are identical, will choose the more expensive because of a confidence factor built solely by advertising.

Client/Agency Loyalty

One of the endless controversies in the world of advertising and marketing is whether an advertiser should form a house agency or enlist the aid of outside counsel.

Here are eight small-space cigar ads. Each positions itself to achieve a specific appeal—technique, price, location, history, origin, sale, gourmet ambiance. Thus, all can coexist in a highly competitive milieu.

Logic would appear to embrace both notions. A house agency is controllable, usually more informed about the company and its products, and less likely to superimpose an outside point of view on the marketing program. It certainly is no paradox to advertising veterans that those same sets of circumstances justify having an outside agency.

With the slow demise of the 15 percent commission tradition, agencies tend to live more on their wits and offer a greater diversity of services than was the case when they were purely media-driven. Media have been a bone in the throat of advertising agencies since the rise of media-buying services, which effectively scuttled the 15 percent formula for compensation.

The typical agency approach is to announce itself as the company's marketing partner. This would seem, at first blush, to be a misnomer, because one of the two partners puts up all the cash. What does the other partner supply? Actually, the term *partnership* is unnecessary. An advertising agency brings a smorgasbord of expertise to the table, including (its clients hope) an independent judgment that helps prevent a campaign from becoming so intramural that it excludes those outside the company.

In an ideal circumstance a client says to the agency, "This is what we have to accomplish." The agency says to the client, "This is how we will accomplish it." Both statements have to be integrity-based, or the partnership soon splits.

Agencies often complain—rightly so—about the lack of client loyalty. Loyalty, though, is no longer a major factor in a serious and money-spending relationship. Consumers have proved this, and the client also can complain—rightly so—that the company's customers have no loyalty.

That an agency has held an account for half a century is of no consequence. The "What have you done for me lately?" syndrome is not only in fashion, it is, in the twenty-first century, completely logical and unassailable. Those who achieved results for this client fifty years ago are no longer directing the agency's creative and media-buying destiny.

Where the worlds collide is in the too-frequent circumstance of an agency being replaced after having done a better-than-creditable job. Actually, according to advertising trade publications, this happens less frequently now than it did in the days of the three-martini lunch and the round of client golf.

The agency J. Walter Thompson has held the Ford account for considerably longer than half a century. Yet the co-president of that agency was quoted as saying—tongue-in-cheek but obviously thoughtfully—

Every morning in the shower I say to myself, "What can happen today to get us fired?" Seriously, though, each and every day there are new challenges and you have to be persistent in solving problems and take nothing for granted.

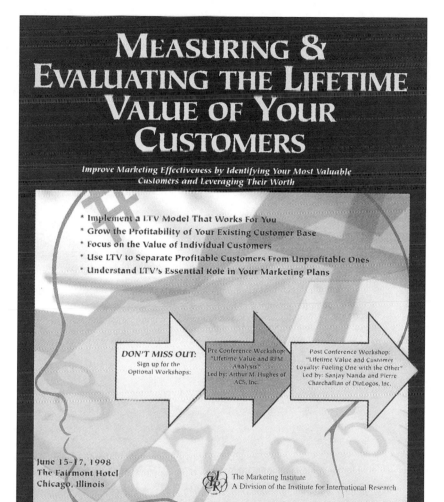

A generation ago, the subject of "lifetime value" might have been worthy of a forty-five-minute speech. In today's loyalty-obsessed marketing environment, a three-day seminar isn't unusual.

Twenty-first-century customer loyalty is directly linked to the "What's in it for me?" syndrome. Loyalty is seldom implicit; it is the by-product of reward, and an entire phylum of reward suppliers exists catering to this burgeoning marketing opportunity.

This executive suggests that the solid relationship between client and agency is built and maintained by traditional values—hard work, persistence, and delivery of more than the client expects.

In an era of MBA-driven, cold-blooded, bottom-line-superconscious corporate structures, loyalty necessarily has to give way to performance. That the result is a synthetic loyalty built on profitability instead of a natural loyalty built on emotional compatibility is the reality of a highly evolved awareness on both partners' part that without performance, loyalty is a liability, not an asset.

The Birth of Some Campaigns

When Quaker Oats Company finally decided to sell its Snapple soft drink brand, the timing was based on the failure of a campaign titled "Escape with Taste." While awareness of the campaign was not in question, sales of the product continued to fall. In one quarter sales were 23 percent below the previous quarter. Survival, at press time, seems to be tied to a campaign concept more likely to generate sales.

McDonald's during this same period, launched a "Campaign 55" program whose failure resulted in its U.S. president/CEO retiring and its advertising agency being placed in jeopardy. Should the agency have disavowed responsibility for the failed campaign? Most industry pundits would regard such a move as cowardice. Failure tests a partnership and often severs it, but that both partners participated should eliminate the capability of one to blame the other.

During this same period, Blockbuster Video, once a dynamic force in advertising, was battling furiously to hold sales at a flat level. The company's apparent inability to do so was often blamed on its acquisition by a larger company, Viacom. But analysts of both advertising and financial disciplines seemed to agree that the market for video rentals was itself in decline and that Blockbuster, for survival in any kind of recognizable form, would have to parallel the tobacco industry in creating peripheral money generators.

A microbrewery, Pete's Wicked Ale, doubled its sales when its promotion agency created a campaign in which baseball fans "got even" for the cynicism displayed by both team owners and players: the "Salary

Cap GreedStakes." The brewer credits the agency with helping to double the sales of Pete's Wicked Ale over the previous year.

A Matter of Fairness

Is it fair for an agency to have to live on its wits, constantly pressured to prove it's a bottomless wellspring of salesmanship? It seems that those on both sides of the agency/client table think it isn't unfair at all. After all, isn't that what agencies are supposed to do?

As one executive on the client side puts it: "My mechanic is supposed to keep my car running. My technician is supposed to keep my computer from crashing. My agency is supposed to keep my sales humming."

Interview with Cliff Einstein

President, Dailey & Associates
Los Angeles

What advice would you give a client who is looking for "the right" agency?
CLIFF EINSTEIN: I think that if a client wants the best possible work from an agency, that client should do the best job they can to hire an organization they respect enough to trust to do things the agency is supposed to be expert at. And the way to find that agency is more than having a bunch of agencies come in and show them speculative work—which will only test how lucky that agency got that week or what freelancers they hired—or how well suited they were to one assignment.

Call companies you admire that seem to be using advertising well. Chief executive to chief executive, ask, "Do you like this company? Do you like that company?" Hire somebody that somebody else likes. Then meet the people to see if they'll fit. Have a long lunch with them. Don't necessarily see them in their own quarters, where they have their own tricks going.

Why does liaison between client and agency so often founder?

C.E.: Let's assume you've hired an agency. Chances are you won't be in charge of the relationship. You'll give that to somebody else, who will be "in charge" of the agency relationship: a marketing director, a series of brand managers, or a series of product managers. The problem will be that you took great pains to hire somebody who fits you. Now you're going to turn the job over to somebody who has no experience doing the job. But in a brand management system, the brand managers you turn it over to are going to read their own handbooks and do all the things those handbooks told them to do or some professor told them to do. And they're going to put too much structure into the relationship, and there are going to be too many approval points.

You've sometimes used the term people with stopwatches in their hands. *Can you explain?*
C.E.: In the classical packaged-goods organizations, you have people with stopwatches in their hands. It's not a tool they're used to using. They never know what to do with those stopwatches. They are determining how early the product name should be mentioned. They're determining what proportion the "fun" part should be and what proportion the "sales" part should be—when in fact the whole thing should be "fun and sell." They are commenting on copy when copy is a component of a sales pitch—and they're commenting on adjectives.

That means you don't trust the resource you've just hired. So you have to tell the people who administrate your advertising that when you agree to the strategy, just make the creatives continually demonstrate that they're on strategy. Don't bother them when it comes to how they will execute that strategy. If it's off-color or in bad taste, if the tonality is something you're not comfortable with, talk about that. But don't tell them what adjectives to use, how loud to talk, what kind of music to use, because you'll make the work stiff.

Pursue being different. Pursue standing out. When work on a job or campaign is finished, if you look at it and don't "get it" quickly, reject it, because no one else will get it.

If you don't understand the consumer because you're not the same age as the consumer, make sure that you have someone in your company that you think does understand the consumer. And let that person be the gateway for the agency. If he or she feels the work fits, then you have to trust that person.

If you don't have that person, then let your agency become the guardian. If you don't trust your agency, then you have the wrong agency. Get another agency.

Why do clients hire agencies and then dictate to them?
C.E.: Those same clients probably hire people and do that, too. That flawed management style probably exists inside their company. They should examine how they grant responsibility.

I think the chief executive should be very involved in the advertising, which is the public posture of his or her company. It's very healthy when the chief executive wants to know all about the advertising. When I see the chief executive come to a film shoot or a music session, I know I've got a remarkably good client. The more a chief executive is interested in what goes into his advertising, the more in touch that chief executive is with his consumer.

How have you structured your agency for maximum efficiency and creativity?
C.E.: I have a strange structure. Since I started my company as its creative director, and since I've been doing that for twenty-nine years in this company, I can't understand why I should turn that final job over to someone else now, unless I'm not good at it. But there's no indication that I'm not good at it. The only weakness I'd have is, Do I speak the language of an age younger than I am? But that doesn't affect strategy and selling propositions; that would just affect voice and tone.

So when it comes to those audiences, I'll ask someone else to craft the voice and tone, and I'll look at it and ask, "Is this in rhythm? Is this smart? Is this communicating?" But many, many of the products that we sell, I'm still a consumer of. So if I think I'm a consumer of something, then I can write the advertising, review the advertising or judge it, or participate in its creation.

If the chief executive is involved in the making of the advertising, he's sending the message that it's an important part of the company, so I think it's OK to be that. I think that's really healthy. And there are some good agencies that have that. Goodby still has that as a quality. Chiat/ TBWA does. Fallon does.

Those are the kinds of agencies who still have the personalities of the people who started them, just as your agency, Dailey, does, aren't they?
C.E.: We're still in our first personality. It's evolved. We make it contemporary and stay young.

But the sense of the agency, the personality of the agency, continues to have continuity with the company that was originally formed. We haven't needed to create a new culture. It's just that the original culture wouldn't quite work today because it's a different time, it's a different era, it's almost thirty years later. But hopefully the people have grown and understand that, too.

So nearly thirty years later, has your relationship building or the way you work with clients changed?
C.E.: No, I always had the most success when I involved the clients in all the processes, so they thought they were an integrated part of the solution. That was very successful for me.

I was shooting commercials for Kaufman and Broad not long ago, and the CEO of the company showed up at the shoot. He had the director, the agency creatives, and the actor to his home for dinner the night between the two shooting days. When he saw the final commercial cut, he knew exactly what it was going to look like. He remembered the scenes. He was watching them being shot on the TV monitor. And when *The Wall Street Journal* last week asked him about his advertising, he could talk all about it. Because he helped make it. That's really efficient when that happens.

I have another client where the work we do is shown quarterly to the CEO by a man who kind of has that as a job. The man who's showing it to the CEO isn't participating in the strategy or the execution; the CEO often has not seen the work before it's shot. Sometimes he's seen something. So when he doesn't like something, it's terrifying because we've already invested production money and everything else into the work. So no one knows what to do with that information.

You then have a campaign that the boss doesn't like, and you live with that for a year?
C.E.: Everybody's depressed. Everybody's demotivated.

Do they ever make you pull it?
C.E.: You can pull it. You might pull it.

Is there any way you can motivate him to get more involved in it? How would you do that?

C.E.: In this case, he didn't start the company. He came up through sales.

I have another big company I work for where the CEO sees everything that's going to be produced, and if he thinks the idea has the wrong tonality or isn't right, he'll nix it in storyboard stage. And whether you like that or not, that saves the agency from the difficulty of "We never should have done this idea."

The thing you don't want in a company is fear. Fear occurs when people are trying to second-guess what will the big boss think after this is done. You're on a shoot. Somebody reads a line a certain way. Everybody is second-guessing what the big boss is going to say about that. So you cover yourself. You spend hours trying to guess what somebody else will like. That's hard work. That means you're not doing work for the consumer, you're doing work to cover your butt. And it's expensive. And it doesn't make good advertising.

Sometimes you can use the system to do very good work. One of my clients is Nestlé Foods, the world's largest food company. We produced work for Alpo this year, relaunching their national brand image. The CEO saw that work in the very roughest of stages, a very simple storyboard. He embraced the idea hugely and let it be known throughout the company that this is a big idea, and he applauded it. That kind of support allowed us to maintain a very pure idea all the way through the subsequent meetings where other people reacted to the work.

If I had my choice, I would show the work to the CEO people first, and the brand people second. But that's structurally not convenient for big companies.

Explain the "big company" attitude versus the "little company" attitude.

C.E.: The more a big company can think like a small company, the more inventive they can become in their communications program.

And yet this seems to be the decade where big companies are thinking like even bigger companies. Big companies are spending so much time organizing so they can administer properly, that they suck the entrepreneurial quality out of the equation.

MBAS seem to have assumed a major position in advertising and marketing. How do you adapt their bottom-line thinking to coincide with marketing goals?

C.E.: I do a three-hour seminar every year at UCLA. I do it for people in a program called the Executive MBA program. These are people already in the marketplace. They are sufficiently important to their company that their companies have paid $50,000 to get them this MBA. They're hand-picked people, twenty-five, twenty-eight, thirty-five years old.

I tell them every year that you have to get up every morning and believe that you run your own little company. All the decisions should be made, if you can, based on what I like, what I do. Not, "How can this come back and bite me? If this doesn't work, will they pin it on me?"

And then you will get advertising solutions that reflect how you look at life. If you're not an entrepreneur, you're going to get deadly dull advertising solutions. If you are entrepreneurial, you will get brilliant advertising solutions.

In an increasingly skeptical consumer ambience, can offbeat marketing still work?
C.E.: I did a candy campaign for a brand named 100 Grand Bar. We had a fabulous, rich idea. The bar was called the $100,000 Bar, which was later changed to the 100 Grand Bar because it was such a rich candy bar. It had chocolate and crunchies and lots of caramel. It's being relaunched. It hadn't been advertised for ten years. We brought them a premise where the theme was very irreverent because the bar is sold to young people. Anything that rich can't be bought by people who are worried by cavities. So we created very irreverent advertising.

Example: There's a beauty contest where a classic, unctuous kind of a host of a beauty pageant says, "And now, for our three finalists, what would you do with a hundred grand?" And the first gal, bubbling over with her little bouffant hairdo, says, "I would sprinkle flower seeds all over the world, so the world would be a better place to live." And the second girl says, "I would buy everyone a puppy, so that we could have the kind of love I feel right now." And the third chick comes up in a simple black dress and short hair—"And what would you do with a hundred grand?"—and she says, "I'd eat it." And everyone goes, "Whoooaaaaaaa!" And then the announcer tells you how cool the bar is and everything that's in it. And then the girl says, "And then I would try to recycle the wrapper." And everyone goes, "Yaaaayyyy."

In another spot a group of old "family" boys, mob guys, sit in what looks like a kitchen out of time in Miami (where Meyer Lansky lived), and they sit at a kitchen table and scheme. One guy says, "So you know it's there?" and the boss says, "It's there. A hundred grand." And another guy says, "What's the split?" And the boss says, "No split. A hundred grand. A hundred grand. A hundred grand." Third guy says, "I can't go in there. They know me." And the boss says, "No. We'll use Sal. Sal! That's beautiful." The announcer tells you about 100 Grand, and Sal, who is Sally, comes in, nine years old, his little granddaughter. She says, "Here, Grandpa." He says, "Thanks, Sally. Keep one for yourself." She spills a dozen 100 Grand Bars on the table.

So we had a young man, not even the boss of the division, realize that this stuff was hot. And he embraced this idea all through the presentation process—and, fortunately, other people liked it as well. This young guy carried it through so strong that the spots stayed pure and the story I just showed you was the original presentation. If I showed you the film, it's word for word the film. And, blessedly, the chief executive of the company thinks it's the neatest thing he's seen. Everybody likes it. That work came out so pure that one might say it shouldn't have got through a large company. But we had an early champion who wasn't a boss but *thought* he was a boss. He had a "command personality." So everybody got lucky.

When you have a big idea, and you know this is what you need to do, how do you approach clients to convince them to become that entrepreneur in their company? How do you convince them to take this ball and run with it? C.E.: When I get one of those very big ideas (and they come infrequently that big) and I literally can smell that they're giant, first, I do everything that I can to ensure that the idea is as big as I thought it was. I try it out on my friends. I try it out on people I respect. I play with it for weeks. I test it. I try to break it down. I make sure the idea doesn't have hidden flaws I didn't know about which would cause the idea to collapse along the way. I make sure it's unique, or at least that it's fresh. When I'm sure I have a real winner, I sit down and put as much effort into the selling process of the idea as I did into, or as some of our people might have done into, the creation of the idea. I plot out a path for selling it. Every idea will need a different path. Since ideas are bought by people, I first have to find the person in the company I'm going to present it to who will have the most affinity for that idea. And I go there. I informally might go to somebody out of the line and salt it. I try to reduce the element of surprise so that it doesn't get "lost by surprise," and I try to get momentum going. I then have to find a way to present it so that I can properly express it.

Are there any rules for presenting ideas like these? What if the presenter isn't a natural storyteller?
C.E.: If you're by nature a storyteller, then you trust yourself, and you can simply present it and tell it. If you're not, then you're going to need some borrowed device—a film or an exemplar. If it's all visual, you may need a visual device; if it's musical, you may need to present the music. So when you have an idea that you feel is a big one, you have to become convinced that this is a good idea that will fit the individual you're selling it to. If you have a match, you should be able to close that sale. And if you don't have a match over there, then you probably aren't going to sell it. If you have important executives at the top of the company who, by nature, aren't going to like this idea, then you shouldn't even bother presenting it, because even if you sell it, it's going to die.

So a "big idea" succeeds only if all parties are in sync?
C.E.: Big ideas are only big ideas if the companies also think they're big ideas. Big ideas improperly produced become small ideas.

If you have to sell a concept, doesn't the agency's client in many ways parallel the eventual advertising target?
C.E.: The first task is selling a product to an audience. My product is my idea. My audience is my client. And I've got to complete that. Then we take that to the consumer. But if I've sold the big idea to the client, but to sell it I've got to make sufficient compromise so that it isn't what it was supposed to be, I'll have a failure. It's got to stay pure enough.

Can you give us an example?
C.E.: We presented the idea of using Tom Skerrett, a wonderful actor, to Kaufman and Broad, to represent their whole company. He was the physical personification of their company. He was sufficiently blue collar, he was incredibly trustworthy, he was every man's man and every woman's man, he was virginal in that he had not presented anyone's story on television, he was incredibly well liked, and he was expensive. At one point it appeared that to sell him, we'd have to say, "He can do

everything for you. He can do all the retail advertising, all this, all that."
But I knew he wouldn't, and he wouldn't do it well. So I had to sell him
with the understanding that he's there to present the soul of the company, not to tell you the price of the house. And if you want him to tell
you the price of the house, then we'll have to get someone else. He
won't be good for that. And the chief executive of Kaufman and Broad
inherently knew that. That's what makes him a rare client. That was very
fortunate. So we got very pure, very effective commercials.

How do you match a celebrity to what that celebrity is supposed to sell?
C.E.: We've had lots of good luck matching celebrities to advertising
brands. The mistake in looking at that from the outside is to think that
what we're doing is hiring celebrities. That's not what we think we're
doing. What we think we're doing is finding the best possible performer
who inherently represents the traits of the brand. Generally, famous
actors are better actors than nonfamous actors. Because they are such
good actors, they got to be famous. So when we introduce a brand with
a famous personality, we are leapfrogging years of education. We are
jumping right to step five in the equation and telling the consumer,
"You know what John Wayne is like, just think that Great Western Bank
is like that. You know what Lindsay Wagner is like, just think that the
Ford dealers are like her." And in Lindsay Wagner's case, it wasn't that
she had the persona as such; it was that she had the ability to play any
number of different roles. So what we really created for her was a television series that's now over fifty commercials in almost ten years. And in
each one, she plays a different role. She's a PTA mom, she's someone
going out with a four-wheel-drive vehicle, she's going to a formal, going
to a dinner, she's somebody who wants an electric car but doesn't know
if she should splurge for one, she's someone who needs an economy car
but wants it to look good, and she plays each of those roles very well,
plays each one a little differently. So she ended up being a great actress
for this series, rather than just "Get a famous person and have that person read lines." So that's what's been good for us.

Dennis Weaver represented Great Western Bank for over ten years.
And he personified trust, continuity, honesty, the simple story, and the
West. And that was an ideal way to fold all that into one symbol and
then express it in advertising.

Do the same "celebrity rules" apply to both broadcast and print?
C.E.: An actor or actress whom you're used to seeing walking and talking is better in television than in print. In print, if you use a model, a model does fine. Often models are worse in television because they don't speak and walk and talk well. Sometimes they do, sometimes they don't. So maybe they're just better off in print. Claudia Schiffer is Claudia Schiffer. I don't want her to talk to me. I don't want Cindy Crawford particularly to talk to me. I just want to look at her. Because that's what she does best.

In your opinion, how will the Internet evolve into good advertising?
C.E.: I think eventually advertising and the Internet will have their own individual marriage. You'll be able to put on the first draft of the commercial that was much too long and had all kinds of interesting little subplots to it and wandered and was very loose and very improvisational. That thing can finally go somewhere. It can go on the Internet. If the idea took a minute and a half, you'll be able to use it. If it only took forty-two seconds, you'll be able to use it. You don't have to fit your idea into any time frame or any form or even any taste level.

Taste level?
C.E.: The taste level is a problem. Categorically, you don't want to start regulating what people can do. But on the other hand, you can't have a product that's so pornographic that you're afraid to turn it on in your home. So I have no idea what we do about that. I think that basically what goes on in the home is the parent's problem, and the parent has to rule the home.

So there has to be some easy way for the parent to be comfortable that the children don't have access to the books the parent keeps on the high shelf the kids can't get to or the pictures the parents keep in the locked drawer. The parents should be able to do that. I think what's frustrating people right now is that the parent cannot control what's going on. The parent can only say, "Don't use my computer. Don't use my television set." So, if you buy a television set today, you can lock out channels. You can keep your porno videotapes in a locked case if that's something you need to do. But you can't control the computer yet. So you're going to have to be able to do that. And it won't be as simple as a lock and a key, because you won't know what there is to lock. There's just too much information.

What do you see as a significant change affecting both the client's way of approaching advertising and the agency's way of approaching advertising?
C.E.: One change that became epidemic in the 1990s: the realization that you could grow a company faster by buying another company than you could by making a product better. And so the sense that merging companies into yours creates managers instead of entrepreneurs. And companies were founded, not on the basis of making something well, not on the basis of "I have an idea, let's start a company" or "I have a service, let's start a company," but "I could put these four companies together, sell off two of them, make a bundle, and have a cash cow working over here, and have a real good operation working over there. Who do I want to run that? A guy from business school that knows about numbers."

That's a bad client. He or she doesn't want the same kind of advertising as somebody who invented a product and wants to tell the world about it. That's what's happened.

What do we do about that?
C.E.: You try to bend those people around to convince them that the consumer will respond more to their product if they do this than if they do that. It's a fantastic experience to look at a set of plans on a new Kaufman and Broad development community and walk through houses, as I did yesterday, using an idea we created. We created a new concept in the community for the empty nester. The houses were built, and we went to a planning meeting. There was a task force. When we looked at what was being presented, we said, "We didn't get there yet. This is too normal. Too expected." We redid the homes. The problem was that they now would cost 15 percent more. But the division president said, "I agree. We'll just figure out what to do with that problem." When we finished the homes, we gave the community a name and a theme that said, "It's like a resort, but it's home." It's not a retirement community. And it's not a community for kids. It's an empty-nester, low-maintenance, incredibly interesting, gated and walled village where you can live with no backyard but a beautiful patio, a front yard that's maintained by the community, a common pool and cabana, and walking

paths. I walked through the models, and I was awed by how exciting they looked. And this would be the advertising, explaining to people how different they were.

Do you think twenty-first-century advertising will be more efficient?
C.E.: We became so mature in business in this country that we got to the point where we had too much of everything. So reduction began to occur in the eighties, and we are continuing to reduce. We're reducing the number of advertising agencies, we're reducing the number of stock brokerages, we're reducing the number of banks and savings and loans, we're reducing the number of insurance companies, we're reducing the number of airlines, we're reducing the number of automobile companies.

Notice, I haven't used the word *increase* once. The first half of the century, I'd have used *increase* for every single subject that I just mentioned. "Decrease" doesn't mean failure. It just means we're cleaning up, we're making things more efficient. Efficiency is not the hallmark of entrepreneurialism. It's the hallmark of managing a business.

Do you envision the role of advertising becoming more recognized in marketing?
C.E.: Advertising too often has been regarded as an expense, rather than a part of marketing. It's factored in as a necessary expense rather than an undeniable part of selling a product. When a company gets in trouble, the first thing cut is advertising, because it affects the bottom line.

When you treat advertising as an expense, as a necessary evil, when the CEO of a company doesn't really believe in advertising but can't figure out how to avoid it, you get bad advertising. When the CEO loves the fact that he can advertise what he made, you get good advertising.

Interview with C. Michael Palmer

Former agency owner; subsequently Executive Vice President, BJK&E Toronto

Agencies have made a big point lately of no longer being media-driven. They want to be a client's marketing partner. What can the agency do out-

*side the area of media that a company's own in-house marketing depart-
ment cannot do?*

MICHAEL PALMER: I'll answer the question from the perspective of a client.
When I was a client, I worked at a quite large major marketing company.
I worked with a lot of advertising agencies—some of the biggest and
the best. A lot of them I admired, and some I didn't admire, but with all
of them there was something lacking in what they brought to the
client's table, which is actually what led me to go into the business. And
the reason it was lacking was because they really didn't understand in all
its nuances the world the clients live in.

Then how did you view the agency function and purpose?

M.P.: We as clients looked upon the agencies as creative resources,
regardless of what service capability they offered. As our creative
resource, it was their role to come up with innovative and creative solutions. It was our role to operate within our systems, to satisfy management's requirements to do all of the budgeting and forecasting, to write
the business plans, to coordinate all of our activity with our plants and
our distribution centers, our sales forces, and so on. We didn't have the
time nor did we have the right kind of environment to think creatively.
Even though we were often charged to do it, it was hard to be creative
in that kind of system.

Did you view agencies as hired hands or as partners?

M.P.: I always thought that the agencies could be contributing so much
more across the spectrum of our business, at least the marketing part of
our business, than simply bringing in what often were great campaigns
with great ideas, but at the same time we weren't getting the benefit of
that kind of creative thinking applied to other parts of the marketing
equation.

For example, how about innovative and unusual sales motivation
programs? How about sales promotion events that really made everything work at retail? A campaign might shift attitudes and build image
for the brand, but a great promotion in retail can really drive the brand.
What is often needed in addition to understanding the environment is
great creative thinking, out-of-the-box kind of thinking. We never got
nearly enough of that from our agencies.

So where did you go to get that kind of marketing creativity?
M.P.: Over the years I probably worked with six or seven major agencies. And when we didn't get this kind of thinking, we hired consultants, we hired sales promotion shops, we hired independents, trying to get this kind of creative thinking. It made it more difficult to bring all aspects of the marketing effort together, working from central strategy and a central theme. If you were trying to do all that yourself, working with many different disparate resources and companies just made the job much more difficult.

So that's the agency management's challenge: It is their job as a communications organization to pull these entities together for the benefit of the brand, for the client's business. And advertising agencies have now realized they have to offer all the pieces of the marketing communications mix.

Has this been a gradual realization?
M.P.: Actually, they realized it quite suddenly, and not because clients demanded it. It was actually diminishing client demand that brought on the realization. The traditional agency business—the media business that built the great agencies and fed them through so many decades—is a diminishing equation, with fragmented media and the inefficiencies inherent in it. Now clients are trying to support their brands through mass communication methods, micromarketing, segmenting of consumers, not just into demographics but into psychographics and lifestyle practice and so on.

That's resulted in an explosion of media sometimes referred to as "new media." Even in traditional media, such as the magazine industry, there's a huge proliferation of specialty magazines of all types and descriptions. The good news is the marketer can now pinpoint targets more and more precisely in order to reach them. The bad news for the agencies: It makes their jobs a lot tougher. It puts their relevance as mass communicators at risk.

Aside from relevance, how has this change affected agency income?
M.P.: This change in communications environment has forced margins. It has placed a huge pressure on traditional agency profit structures. It has forced a reaction of technology to make the business more efficient and, therefore, profitable again. And, of course, along with that chang-

ing environment, there comes the need to start building all of these other skills and communication disciplines into the agency organization.

Speaking of changes in environment, you've been involved in several agency mergers, and you've been charged with helping to bring separate cultures together. How do you unify different agencies while keeping the esprit de corps intact?

M.P.: I'll start with the "what happens": First of all there is fundamental impending change coming, and everybody in the agency knows that before the merger actually happens. That creates a whole bunch of emotional reactions.

There's apprehension. There's excitement. Because while people resist change, they also want change. It's schizophrenic. Change energizes them, so the apprehension comes from not knowing; the excitement comes from anticipating. This can be good. That's the starting point. When the cultures come together, the dynamics start happening very, very rapidly. It's like a chain reaction, and every reaction is heightened. Everyone exaggerates the differences because everyone in that "other" culture is different from what your value system is or what your culture is.

And the comparative reactions?

M.P.: Your reaction can either be critical, or envious, or admiring. If there's a lot more power on one side than on the other side, you're going to have a fairly major problem, because one culture is simply going to eat up another culture—unless there's a real purpose that has been articulated to the whole group.

For example, when we were still a relatively young agency in Toronto, independently owned, we were approached by the Canadian operation of a large global agency. They weren't winning new business, they were losing business. They weren't attracting the best talent in the business. They were looking for a solution. They were interested in us even though we were a lot smaller.

They were interested in buying us not for the normal reasons (the normal reasons being "Let's make ourselves bigger, let's make ourselves stronger, let's add skills"), they were interested in buying us because they thought we could energize their agency. Because we were a young agency, we were coming up with unconventional solutions. We were doing some pretty outrageous stuff. We were feisty and outspoken, and they were convinced that we could energize their business. I actually felt that in spite of their good intentions, it wouldn't have worked. In the end they would have swallowed us.

Another experience: Our young, feisty agency eventually became part of a major global network, and we were asked to absorb the local office of this global agency into our agency. We in this case were the bigger agency in the market. We were three times the size they were in terms of buildings and people, and we had seen all of the nightmare of mergers around us for many, and we said, "By God we're not going to let it happen to us."

So we got together as a management team and divided up responsibilities for managing this merger. One of us was responsible for communication; one of us was responsible for counseling, guiding new people coming into the organization; another was responsible for managing all the physical aspects of the merger. We thought we did everything right—and it was a disaster. Twenty new people came into a sixty-person shop, and twelve months later two of the twenty were still there. That's because the cultures were too different, and we didn't recognize how different. Work ethics, operating philosophies, the management principles—every one of these was like day and night. Obviously, as the larger entity and the managing entity, we just assumed right from the beginning that they would accept our values as good values because we were very successful in the marketplace.

They didn't.

So I thought back on that experience, wondering how could we have allowed that to happen, and figuring out what I would have done differently. First, I would have sized up the two cultures to a much greater extent. Then I would have intensely interviewed all of the people, and I simply would not have taken in the people who were not prepared, honestly and sincerely, to give our culture a good shot. That way, we could probably have saved a fair amount of agony and disruption.

If they were so unprepared and the fit was so poor, what was the value of the merger?

M.P.: Another observation I make is on the subject of purpose: The only purpose of that merger was convenience. There should be a bigger purpose attached to any merger.

If you see that you can add all the core elements and core strengths of all the merging agencies and you can clearly come up with a whole that's stronger than the sum of the parts, that's a logical purpose for merger. If you don't have that starting point, you have no point to a merger.

▪ 3 ▪

Budgeting

A major function of the advertising agency is to spend the client's money. That's the first half of the statement. The second half: *and* to spend it wisely and effectively.

The agency whose first question of a prospective client is "What's your budget?" is in trouble, whether the agency knows it or not. "What's your budget" should follow "What's your goal?"

How Much Will It Take?

Historically, determination of budget has been the result of one of three procedures:

1. Analysis, scientific or empirical (the "task" approach)
2. Copying what the competition is doing
3. Fiat

Obviously, the first is the most scientific; but for that very reason, it may be the least effective. A predetermined budget carries with it the burden of inflexibility. In the post-future-shock era, contingencies are more common than uninterrupted progress. Still, analysis-based budgets have, quite properly, dominated the procedural field.

Basing a budget on what the competition is doing also generates an implicit problem; the technique is based on *reaction* rather than on aggressive action. A paradox: The very nature of a competition-based budget makes the procedure of creating it by far the most aggressive procedure. A benefit is that, of the three methods, it most positively gears itself to the competitive nature of the marketplace.

Fiat-based budgets are the bane of media people who want a budget to be based on reality rather than emotion. Since the publication more than half a century ago of the book *The Hustlers,* the image of a cranky CEO snarling, "This is how much we're going to spend," has occasionally been fact rather than fiction. But this method, too, has a benefit: Not only is the budget arrived at quickly, but if the dictator has immersed himself or herself in the marketplace, it may actually be the most accurate method of all.

How Much Difference Can Another $100 Million Make?

The marketing publications constantly report on preannounced budgets. Where do those numbers come from? For example, when Pizza Hut was planning a "repositioning campaign," the announced budget was $200 million. The bulk of that budget was dedicated to television, featuring the president of Pizza Hut, an apparent move in the common direction started some years ago by Lee Iacocca, then the head of Chrysler. The technique, sometimes valid and sometimes purely ego-driven, has been to make a recognizable celebrity out of an otherwise anonymous executive. Was this a component of the $200 million determination?

Equally possible and equally logical was the realization that any consumer will spend a finite amount of money at fast-food restaurants, and the most memorable may be the most visited. McDonald's, switching its advertising agency at the same time Pizza Hut launched its repositioning campaign, had an announced budget of $300 million. Obviously, a national budget of $10 million would not have been competitive. The dedicated amount, it would seem, was dictated by a combination of all three budget procedures

The Fallacy of "Behaviorism"

The year was 1919. A relatively unknown, until that point, psychologist named John Watson published a book titled *Psychology from the Standpoint of a Behaviorist*. The behaviorist concept, reduced to its most basic explanation, is that an individual's actions are the result and total of the life experiences from birth to that point. For marketing, behaviorism suggested that the human mind is a blank slate at birth. Whoever writes the most on that slate will generate the greatest amount of reaction.

A disciple of Watson in the 1930s was a man named George Washington Hill, head of the American Tobacco Company. That individual adopted the Watsonian concept and relentlessly pounded a slogan into the American consciousness: "L.S.M.F.T." These initials represented, "Lucky Strike Means Fine Tobacco." Did this slavish adherence to behaviorism catapult Lucky Strike cigarettes to a dominant position? No. Another brand, Camel, was on top and stayed on top throughout the assault.

From a marketing point of view, behaviorism has one flaw: It doesn't work. Probably the reason it is so easy to adopt is that it simplifies the campaign. Probably the reason it doesn't work is that mere repetition in itself, while mnemonic, cannot compete with a dynamic call to action.

Camel's campaign was itself geared somewhat to a memorable theme not tied to a call to action: "I'd walk a mile for a Camel." Once dominant, the brand used "Outsells All Other Cigarettes by Billions." This reflected another philosophy of marketing—the bandwagon approach—which McDonald's adopted in its early days: "Over 1 Million Sold." That number increased in the company's advertising until it ran well into the billions.

The McDonald's slogan "You deserve a break today" could not have built the company's commanding position without an accompanying dynamic incentive tied to it. So in its expansion period, this marketer added devices—each heavily supported in its national budget—to initiate and consolidate its competitive position among specific target groups.

For children, the company introduced the character Ronald McDonald; for budget buyers, regular price incentives. A temporary lapse had the company using a stern, forbidding actor, the late John Houseman, as spokesperson. Children were repelled by what appeared to be a haughty, intellectualized image as the jarring replacement for gentle Ronald McDonald. The campaign was quickly dropped.

A problem much television advertising creates for itself is dependence on behavioristic repetition without the necessary dynamism. The dedication of budgeting dollars, in an endless competitive marketplace in which opponents quickly use their own budgets to take advantage of a gap in customer or client attraction, has to have both eyes on improved, or at least retained, market share.

The Paradox of Anticipation

Anticipating results is one of the more inexact nonsciences. "We'll spend $40 million on this" works if the combination of research and educated/uneducated guesses doesn't run afoul of changing (or lacking) acceptance by the intended targets—or if a competitor doesn't charge into the arena with guns blazing.

This may be why a *reactive* budget can outproduce a *proactive* budget. The problem with a reactive budget can parallel the problem of a chess player who matches the previous move by his or her opponent. (This player will announce "Checkmate" one move after the opponent announces "Checkmate.") The challenger, however aggressive, still faces an uphill fight for market share.

Budgeting for Interactive Media

Of all media, interactive represents the greatest challenge because its future is so much more speculative than can be said of any other medium. For example, an organization called Strategic Futures fore-

Budgeting ■ 61

cast in 1997 that spending on interactive advertising will increase from the 1997 level of less than $1 billion per year to $42 billion by the year 2010.

On what was this based? The president of Strategic Futures explained it as the result of a major realignment of advertising and media usage. He said the greater part of this revenue will be from interactive television, which he estimated would reach 35 percent of "wired homes" by 2005.

If you are reading these words in the year 2005 or beyond, was he right? Was his estimate speculation or educated guess? Predicting in the face of ongoing electronic developments—i.e., high-definition television, which, as originally announced, would split television viewership into two discrete camps—has such a high rate of variables as to be accurate or inaccurate by accident, no matter who does the predicting.

The other principal element of interactive, the Internet, is another enigma. With Web sites coming on-line by the tens of thousands every month and others dropping off, the future of this development as an advertising medium is, similarly, subject to wild speculation. Unquestionably, the volume of marketing dollars, pounds, yen, francs, lira, and marks shifted into this medium will increase, if only because the medium itself expands so enormously.

You can see that the uncertainty surrounding interactive media has a spillover effect on all other media. Finite budgets borrow, appropriate, or steal money from one dedication to another. Substituting interactive media for more traditional media in many cases becomes an impenetrable puzzle when preanalyzed years ahead.

The Shifting Sands of Agency Compensation

A handful of advertising agencies—call them "lucky"—still command a 15 percent commission from media as their principal means of compensation. For most, the 15 percent factor has joined the passenger pigeon and the dodo bird in the Great Beyond. Media-buying services have obsoleted what once was thought to be an unbreakable clamp holding client and agency together.

The twenty-first-century agency invariably announces that it shares the goal of its clients: to maximize the use of marketing monies. Without the 15 percent, an agency today is hard-pressed to equal the net return that would have accrued with the traditional commissions.

The result has been that agencies are adding revenue by internal accretion. Agencies add public relations arms, interactive specialists, direct-marketing adjuncts, sports and event marketing, sales promotion departments, corporate identity designers, health and medical divisions, and any other activity contributing to either image or sales.

The subresult of this result has been an almost total reliance on fees rather than commissions. For the agency, this may well be a move upward rather than sideways. Eliminating the most "passive" element in the compensation mix has to mean greater dependence on talent, creativity, and results. This lifts the agency that can perform above the milieu in which competition used to rest, too often, on a base of partially rebated commissions. A 1997 article in *Advertising Age* by a marketing executive condensed the problem to these words:

> *There is an erosion of confidence in advertising that—when coupled with an erosion in margins, in marketing budgets and, more subtly, in the client's confidence in the agency's ability to manage its store properly—will ultimately dictate the terms and the atmosphere of compensation discussions.*

As more and more clients struggle to find a mutually acceptable fee arrangement, more and more clients are militating for fees tied to results. Fair or unfair?

- Fair—if the agency's participation is not constantly second-guessed, changed, and discarded.
- Unfair—if the agency is charged with producing business for a product or service that is impossibly priced or obsolete.
- Fair—because results are the direct responsibility of those who generate response-initiating messages.
- Unfair—because the message alone is but one facet of the marketing mix. Distribution (or its lack) can scuttle an otherwise successful campaign.

An iconoclastic practice, obviously agency-originated, is tying the fee to a percentage of sales. The agency becomes a commission sales person, just as representatives in the field are compensated based on a percentage of sales. Can such a relationship work? Yes, if both parties enter the arena with clean hands, avoid the "Hollywood-style" accounting systems, and agree to a fairly long-term commitment.

The slow death of the 15 percent formula already has shown some nasty fallout. Agencies pitch an account based on a lowball fee and then, almost immediately, complain about being underpaid.

The client who shops for bargains deserves the hungry agency that offers a bargain. This is not to say that paying the most is assurance of getting the best talent and attention. Rather, it is a warning to both parties that success for both has to be the result of linkage based on mutual trust and the absence of fear that speaking with candor will result in termination of the relationship.

One agency's philosophy of compensation is reproduced in Appendix B on page 213.

On What Is a Fee Based?

An archaeologist, 500 years from now, digging up records of a typical advertising agency's bookkeeping in the year 2000, might be nonplussed. "What was all the fuss about?"

One would think that billing for time could be semiautomated. After all, n agency staff, whose time is billed at x, y, or z dollars per hour, performed specific functions for which the agency's client was billed.

As any contemporary agency accounting department will testify, it not only isn't that simple, it isn't the way agencies actually bill. A group of agency people attends either a planning session, a creative session, or, for that matter, a meeting with the client. Are all those people necessary? Should the time of all of them be billable?

Another circumstance: The agency's copywriter/art director team comes up with an execrable idea, which is quickly shot down in flames. A second team is then assigned to the project. Should the client be billed for the first team's useless effort?

Agencies typically total the amount of time all involved personnel have devoted to a job, and then make a determination: Was it profitable or unprofitable? You can see the possibility of a false determination based on the agency's own efficiency.

We see accounts being resigned because their agencies say it was unprofitable to handle them. Internal budgeting is an inexact science. That some agencies operate on a not-for-profit level is not intentional.

Contingency Planning

A headline in the trade newspapers announces that the manufacturer of an imported automobile has set a budget of $250 million. Obviously a budget of that size isn't arrived at accidentally. Suppose the target sales figure is 100,000 cars. This means the manufacturer intends to achieve this goal at an advertising cost of $2,500 per car. The combination of history and experienced marketing executives make the numbers logical enough.

Now, suppose, six months into the model year, only 30,000 cars have been sold. The orgasmic thrust that accompanies new-product introduction and consumer excitement has dissipated, as has 50 to 60 percent of the budget. The factory is grinding out cars at the predetermined clip. Is it time for reevaluation and implementation of a contingency plan?

Yes—if a contingency plan exists. Situations such as this, without a contingency plan, highlight the disadvantage of budget declaration by fiat. Had the company sold 80,000 cars in this same period of time, again a contingency plan might be in order—however, one less crucial than exists when projections are not met.

What might the contingency plan be? Raw dollars are a means, not an end. If the combination of industry history and executive experience has failed to produce the projected results, why should this team assume the allocation of more money will accomplish what the original plan didn't?

So it may be that more money, above the original budget, is called for and should be part of a predetermined contingency. What remains to be decided is the reason the original plans failed to meet projected numbers. Was it a wildly successful product introduction or inventive campaign by a competitor? Was it market conditions that damaged sales projections for all competitors? Was it market rejection of the make and/or model?

The contingency plan has to anticipate all possible circumstances, including exceeding the projections. In that case the contingency plan might be either to reduce the budget for the second half of the model year, stay with the budget and be corporate heroes by out-selling the projection (and, in some corporate structures, by spending all the money allocated), or add monies to consolidate and intensify the increased share of market, which can have a spillover lasting for years to come.

Only masters of corporate espionage can anticipate what a competitor will do to damage a sales projection. In the case of automobile manufacturers, sudden rebates, early introduction of a model year, or a new model that brings a competitor into a previously well-defined arena can destroy a well-planned budget.

But a budget that includes a host of thoughtful contingencies is far more likely to be bulletproof enough to enable the individuals behind it to survive for another battle.

How Client and Agency Agree on Budget Planning

The title of this subhead may be an oxymoron. A budgeting "agreement," like the budget itself, may result from the client's executive fiat.

If the agency is charged with creating a budget and does so with arrogant contempt for market research, the agency has no right to criticize executive fiat because that is exactly what the agency has perpetrated, even if the budget is the result of input by fifty different people.

Proper agency acceptance of responsibility for budget generation stems from preacceptance—after intelligent and candid discussions by both parties—of the intended result of the campaign. This should come from the client, not from the agency, because results are the core of corporate responsibility.

The agency then amasses its forces, primarily media, to determine how much exposure is necessary to achieve these results. As has been proved hundreds of thousands of times (including the discussion of behaviorism in these pages), exposure is no assurance of attention, and attention is no assurance of positive action. So, following intelligent media determinations, the creative staff assumes the responsibility for maximizing the magical combination of attention and desire that results in sales.

Of course, regardless of budget, that should be everyone's intention. This means an injection of statesmanship for all parties involved in the decision-making process. That one department head is enamored of television, another of the World Wide Web, and a third of direct mail should be secondary to a common goal: achieving the results that have been predetermined in that first agency/client budget determination meeting.

The Client's Job/The Agency's Job

Budget is a delicate area for determining what the client's job is and what the agency's job is. In a perfect world, goals would be identical. But the structure of business is such that when one partner is spending money and the other partner's income depends on the amount of money spent, the world becomes imperfect.

The days are long since past when the agency's first question was, "What's your budget?" Yet the dedication of individuals and their time necessarily is geared to that question—which has to arise at some point, not only in the original negotiations, but as each campaign and subcampaign is formed.

Both sets of jobs are, really, truisms. The client's job is to squeeze and maximize returns per dollar, yen, mark, franc, shilling, or peseta spent. The agency's job is one of implementation. A parallel might be a company structuring a new corporate headquarters, allocating a specific amount of money to get the building up, and then hiring a contractor who guarantees that the building will be finished on time and within budget.

What's missing? The architect.

This is where the jobs merge, overlap, and scramble. Both parties are principals of the architectural firm that designs the structure the company wants and the contractor must build.

The agency that doggedly stands on the sidelines, waiting for the budget to be dumped into its lap, has abandoned the architectural role. In such circumstances—not unusual in agency/client relationships—invariably the agency's posture sags and is weakened even if, after all the money is spent, the sales projection is reached.

So the agency's job transcends intelligent spending of somebody else's money. Obviously, the agency (like its client) has to keep an eye on the bottom line. But equally obvious is the mandate for professionalism, and professionalism and untempered greed are poor bed partners.

Witness the agency/client relationships that have endured for twenty years or more. Invariably, these relationships have survived because the agency has been a co-architect as well as the general contractor. Whenever this type of relationship has not existed, accounts have been in jeopardy.

(The Revolving Door Syndrome of the last generation sometimes unfairly strikes an architect-oriented agency, which falls victim to cronyism, the unreasoning desire for change, or market conditions more properly blamed on the client. That does not affect the validity of optimally tended relationships.)

The client's job is to generate a realistic budget that includes flexible components so the campaign can fire competitive salvos effectively when or if the market or competitive conditions change.

Pay for Results: The Next Generation of Budgets?

In an interview quoted in *Advertising Age,* the chief executive officers of DDB Needham and Young & Rubicam explained their enthusiasm for what was originally considered outrageous, then iconoclastic, then alternative, and, eventually, an increasingly accepted technique of agency compensation.

How does the agency budget its own resources when compensation is geared to results? Answer: The key, for these giant agencies at least, is that although projections are constantly at risk, compensation has a floor. What is risked is profit, not operating expenses.

Answering the question "How should the client budget for the variable factors?" one of these executives said his agency tells his clients to budget for the best results; the upside of this type of budget is that if goals are not met, the client saves money from that budget. But under no circumstances is the budget allocation to the agency an all-or-nothing proposition.

An agency of any substance implicitly knows its cost factors. Being paid for performance, with the "if" factor tied to profit beyond raw operating cost and overhead, cannot result in a loss. An unsuccessful campaign (or performance) can only result in a breakeven project.

For example, client and agency agree: The agency will get a payment of 2 percent of its total cost factor for each 1 percent of market share the client's product picks up. The agency's cost for producing the materials is, say, $5 million. The $5 million is guaranteed. As a result of the campaign, the client's market share increases by 3 percent. The agency then is paid an additional $300,000. This may not seem to be comparable to a commission-based arrangement, in which raw cost would be marked up 17.65 percent (to equal 15 percent of the gross), for a commission of $882,500. But the benefits are two:

1. The commission arrangement does not and cannot assure coverage of the agency's costs.
2. The performance payment goes straight to the bottom line.

Another example might be one in which the agency's performance payment becomes a percentage of the *client's* gross or net profits. This is a far more complicated set of formulas, because the agency ties itself to a circumstance over which it has no control. "Creative bookkeeping," while certainly not as prevalent as one might see in individual contracts with movie studios, still is a possibility; a more disastrous possibility is acrimony stemming from arguments over what constitutes profit. Obviously, even if the numbers are adjusted so they appear to be parallel, the agency is better off tying its performance payment to gross profits than to net profits. If the client is a public company, the numbers, too, are public; if the client is a privately held company, the potential for aggressive auditing may give pause to both parties.

What becomes clear in any analysis of a performance-payment relationship is the need for both parties to understand that the relationship is long range, not subject to quick cancellation because of temporary setbacks, and immune from either party feeling exploited because the agreement has not been overly favorable to that party.

Commenting on the pay-for-results arrangement, *Advertising Age* said:

> *What this means for agencies is a willingness to share in some of the risks of their client's business. Putting a chunk of profit at risk is an uncomfortable leap for some in the agency business, but clients take those risks all the time. . . . When advertiser and agency sensibly share risks and rewards, isn't that a big step toward rebuilding the "partnership"?*

The number of agency/client relationships that have foundered on the financial reefs of what constitutes logical compensation is probably beyond estimation. The principal reason is that we have a partnership in which one partner spends the money. Agencies should neither apologize for their fiduciary philosophy nor yield to any temptation based on greed, overstaffing, or the assumption of client naivete. Clients who squeeze their agencies will too often generate either a constant turnover or a nasty reputation, which will cause the best-qualified agencies to avoid them.

So the logic of the client/agency partnership should be obvious: Both parties act with the sincerity and honor a true partnership demands.

Marketing Checklist

1. Is your budget determined by goal, competition, or fiat?
2. If your budget is dictated by goal, is the goal realistic and founded in valid market information?
3. If your budget is dictated by competition, are you certain of competitors' market share and future plans?
4. If your budget is dictated by fiat, are you sure that you have excluded ego and irresponsible personal desire from the decision?

5. Have you made contingency plans flexible enough to be implemented at any point at which the budget seems either unrealistic, insufficient, or improperly aimed?
6. Do your original plans include aiming part of your budget at speculative targets?
7. Does your original budget include maximum flexibility for its portion aimed at speculative targets?
8. Are you prepared to intensify implementation if speculative target groups respond (and withdraw quickly if they don't)?
9. If you are a client, have you structured your financial relationship with your agency to ensure that the best people will be working on your account without having the agency feel it is underpricing its services?
10. If you are an agency, are you positive that the compensation to which you have agreed is adequate—but not overpriced, which may cause client defection?
11. Have you considered a pay-for-results agreement?
12. Is your agency/client agreement structured so that it will survive if the agency is excluded from media commissions?

Interview with Valentine Zammit

Executive Vice President, True North Communications Inc.
New York

We're hearing a lot about fee versus commission agency compensation, and we're hearing about the disappearance of the 15 percent commission. How do you see this developing in the future?

VALENTINE ZAMMIT: Over the last ten years we've seen a huge shift from commissions to fees. And, frankly, agencies have learned to live with this change. More interestingly, over the last five years many clients have expressed interest in compensation tied to product performance in the marketplace.

The problem with performance-based systems is that clients want you not only to take the risk of doing a good job but also to share the risk of the product's success—whether or not success or failure is related to the advertising. Often there are subjective and objective hurdles you have to overcome, and performance becomes very difficult to measure fairly or accurately. It's a controversial subject, but a lot of companies want to explore the performance-based option, so I think it will remain an important issue.

Of course, the far more common fee system is a fixed, negotiated monthly fee. Basically, a flat fee is arrived at based upon an estimate of what an agency's costs will be, including overhead plus a fixed profit percentage. We then present this to the client as the fee. We don't reconcile any overage or underage because we're working on a flat fee. Other arrangements require periodic reconciliation and, depending upon the variances, fee adjustments. As you can see, there's no end to the possibilities.

What about the "cost-plus" method?
V.Z.: The "cost-plus," billing method is based upon billing the hours worked. Actual hours are billed at the end of each month or estimated and negotiated in advance and billed at a standard monthly amount. Then, at the end of a period (as often as quarterly), you reconcile billing against actual hours. The key here is that you want to be able to earn a 20 percent gross profit. Unfortunately there are a lot of clients who don't necessarily agree with that. They think you should earn 15 percent or 10 percent. But if you take a look at the profits of huge corporations today, 20 percent is quite reasonable.

Another thing you have to be careful of when you start talking about profit as a percentage of revenue is that agencies are very different from manufacturing companies. Our revenues are *after* pass-through (cost of goods sold), so our percentage of 20 percent seems much higher than a manufacturing company's return on sales—which is before cost of goods sold. Take a look at a manufacturing company and you'll often see profits of 3 percent or higher before taxes. However, that's equivalent to a 20 percent profit when you eliminate the cost of goods sold from your revenues. Put media costs into our gross sales and we're in the same 3 percent range—if we're lucky.

And other compensation possibilities?
V.Z.: Fee-based compensation systems come in all shapes and sizes. Commission rates remain popular, but the once standard 15 percent commission rate is rare. Today you get a lot of commission systems with

sliding scales: Smaller budgets still yield the higher commission rate, but as you go up the revenue ladder, the commission rate decreases.

Unfortunately, fee-based systems create what I call a "micrometer mentality" among clients. They want to measure everything—very finitely. That means the focus becomes misdirected. The focus should be, "What's the best campaign? What's the best creative? How do we increase sales, share, and profit?" Instead it becomes all that plus the administrative focus: "How many hours did you spend on this project? Did you really have to bring the whole hockey team to the meeting?" An agency becomes ineffective once the focus shifts from quality and results to costs. In the old days, under the commission system, if a client had a problem, he'd call up and say, "Hello, Val, I've got this problem. Will you put a team to work on it?" Now what often happens is he thinks twice about calling. He starts wondering, "If I call they're going to spend at least five hours, five hours times the hourly rate is going to cost me . . . well maybe I shouldn't call." And that's how great advertising ideas never get born. It's very shortsighted for clients to worry more about fees than the results they need and the resources they have available for a particular assignment. So it comes down to this micrometer mentality, which is very dangerous to their business because they end up having the tail wagging the dog.

I had one situation where the client had to do some research and the research cost $10 thousand. The advertising budget was something like $40 million and the client said, "Well, we know the research is important, but we're going to pass on it because it's $10 thousand." I said to them, "Hey, guys, you're going to pass on a $10 thousand investment that could drive $40 million worth of business? If this is important, we should do it."

But why are clients developing what you call a "micrometer" mentality?
V.Z.: I guess it's because they fear that agency people may recommend spending more, so they can make more commission and more profits. It's a problem of trust, and it started back in the '60s and '70s—when agencies were doing very well profitwise. Then when we got into the '80s and '90s, after all the junk bond deals, there was more need for accountability—and accountability comes down to cost-plus analysis.

Can you give us a formula for fee negotiations?

V.Z.: Knowing your costs and estimating them accurately are the critical steps. The formula is very simple: Take the base salary and divide by sixteen hundred hours. That gives you the base hourly rate without overhead. Then you have to determine your overhead rate, and that's a combination of these factors:

1. Your non-charged hours
2. Your indirect salary
3. All your occupancy costs
4. Other standard overhead items

Put the overhead factor on top of the first number—the base hourly rate. Then you take these total costs, and if you want to earn 20 percent profit, you simply multiply the total by 125 percent. That will give you the total rate to be applied against the hours that are being charged.

What is the logical, ethical, and productive step an agency should take if it decides it's losing money on the relationship?
V.Z.: Basically you have to make sure you have the proper documentation to prove your case, and that requires a good cost-accounting system. Get your facts in order based on the cost-accounting system and go to a client and say, "Look. Here are the hours that we charged, here's what our total costs were, and here are the commissions we earned (or the fee that you paid us). There's a problem here: We're losing money."
And then you sit down and negotiate. It's as simple as that.

What compensation method strikes you as most logical in today's environment?
V.Z.: I don't think we should focus so much on going from fixed commissions to sliding-scale commissions or to fees. Instead, I'd rather we concentrated on improving the concept of performance-based compensation. However, if the agency is going to take risks, there must be an opportunity for significant offsetting rewards.

On another financial subject: When should an agency look for a merger partner?
V.Z.: An agency should look for a merger partner, depending upon the size of the agency, under the following circumstances:

1. When the agency doesn't have all the capabilities it needs to service and grow with its current clients
2. When the agency does have all the services, but they are below par—for example they need to improve creative or media or direct marketing
3. When the agency doesn't seem to be getting much attention or getting invited into "pitches," often due to lack of critical mass
4. When the agency lands a client that does business in different states or different locales and the agency has inadequate geographical coverage—so it may need to acquire a company
5. When the agency wants to be global—and many larger agencies must be global—then the agency has to buy affiliates in different countries

But doesn't a circumstance exist in which an agency just decides to buy another agency or be bought by another agency?

V.Z.: Bottom line, the agency must prepare an acquisition strategy that is first and foremost in the best interest of current and future clients and shareholders. You have observed that many major agencies are making acquisitions that do not appear to be very strategic. I suspect that these agencies are feeding the beast to maintain a 15 percent growth rate and satisfy the security analysts. This is very worrisome. I'm not sure how these acquisitions address our number one question, "What's in it for our clients?"

There are very special circumstances where there's no apparent urgent need to make an acquisition, but an opportunity comes along that is so financially compelling that it makes sense. In this case, you can really benefit from synergies—meaning that when you merge two companies instead of two production departments, you will combine them into one. Frequently, when you eliminate duplication, a lot of income drops to the bottom line.

Or there are times where an agency is not financially sound but has a significant client. Then you may want to go in and buy the agency and bring it under your management. Properly structured, you're off to the races.

When you acquire subsidiaries, what do you look for and how should an agency evaluate the work of a particular subsidiary?

V.Z.: Obviously we take a look at the client list. We try to make sure that the revenues are spread over a number of clients. You want to try to avoid buying an agency with one or two clients that represent 80 percent of the gross income. That can become a problem—if one of those clients leaves, the agency is in big trouble.

Those kinds of risks can be reflected in negotiating the acquisition price—and the related warranties and guarantees. You can pay less up front, with the balance over a period of time. You tell the principals of the agency you're buying, "As long as these clients stay, you'll get your payments. If they leave, then in effect I bought something that's worth a lot less, so you're going to get less."

Mightn't an agency buy another agency because of talent?
V.Z.: I surely hope so. Obviously you take a look at the talent and the creative product. In simplest terms, we only buy three things: revenue, relationships, and intellectual equity. They are all hard to find and hard to hold on to—but true intellectual equity is the rarest and most important quality we search for.

▪ 4 ▪

Creative Strategy

The arrival of the World Wide Web as a competing medium of advertising has brought fresh attention to a concept dating from the 1960s: positioning.

The best-known early demonstration of positioning, still quoted in speeches and textbooks, was the tire maker Goodrich, who referring to the Goodyear Blimp, advertised, "We're the other guys." This was positioning at its clearest interpretation.

Positioning: Breaking Through the Clutter

Positioning is out of fashion with many advertising agencies today. Some campaigns espouse the internal gospel that advertising is an end, not a means. As the number of messages to the typical recipient—consumer or business—increases each year, positioning seems to be reestablishing itself as the logical means of combining two goals:

1. Breaking through the clutter
2. Causing the cash register or telephone to ring

One catalyst in this revival of attention to positioning has been the World Wide Web on the Internet. Getting attention was the original goal for the early Web sites; in fact, marketers kept score by the number of "hits," raw landings on the site undefined by further exploration. As sophistication upgraded the medium, it became apparent to both analysts and advertisers that the difference between raw advertising and well-cooked marketing lay in conversions, not hits. So billing methods now are geared to actual inquiries or sales, not hits.

To an automobile dealer, effective advertising is that which brings serious buyers into the showroom. To a fast-food franchisee, effective advertising is that which brings diners into the restaurant. Positioning may be founded on a number of credible bases:

- Price
- Unique combination of benefits
- Length of warranty
- Corporate history
- Claim of anticipated results
- To be determined

"Free" offers, sweepstakes, and coupon promotions provide a temporary position midway between price and the standard motivator, greed. Some consumer products maintain their position almost solely through couponing in freestanding inserts placed in newspapers. In 1993, the giant packaged-goods company Procter & Gamble startled the twin worlds of supermarkets and P&G competition by announcing total positioning based on Every Day Low Pricing (EDLP).

Exploring the USP

Many who give lip service to the philosophy of the Unique Selling Proposition ignore, in practice, the middle word: *Selling.* Without a sales hook, an ad or campaign may have a unique proposition, but it is crippled by lack of selling.

The difference between unique propositions and unique selling propositions parallels the difference between clerks and salespeople

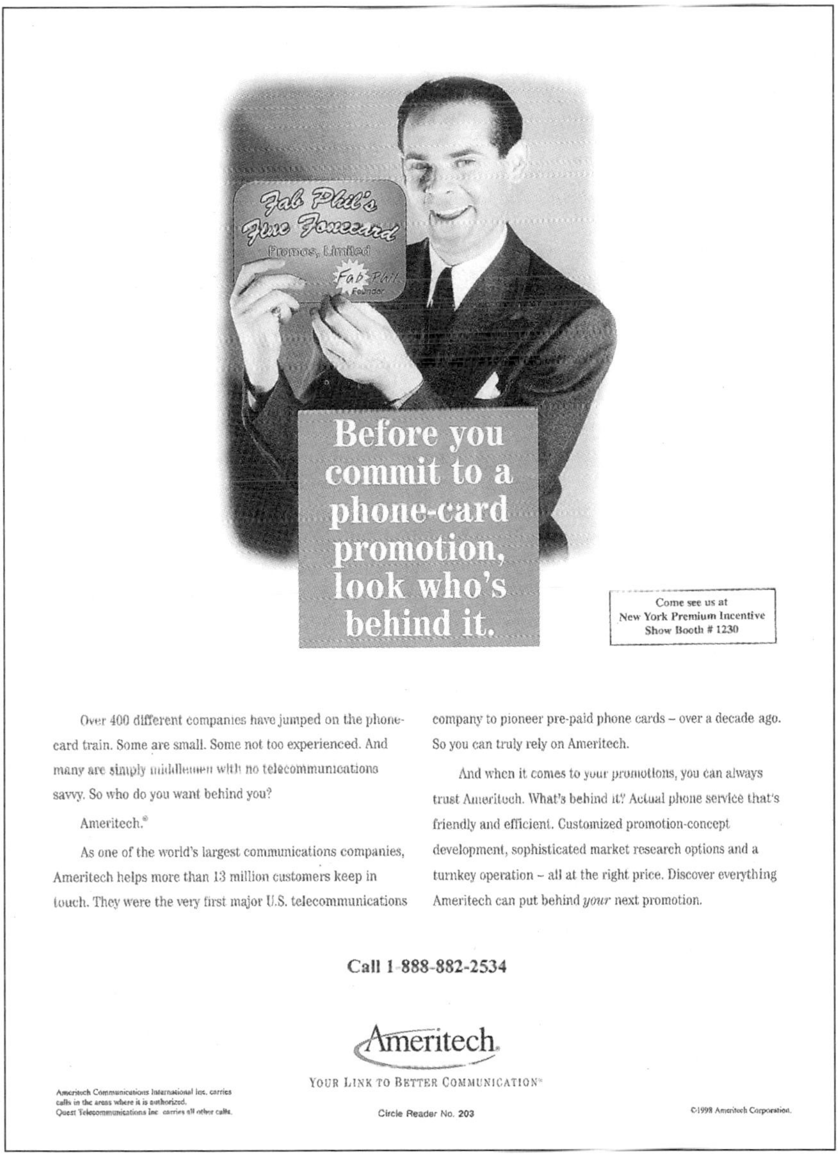

Fab Phil's
Fine Fonecard
Promos, Limited
Fab Phil
Founder
Before you commit to a phone-card promotion, look who's behind it.
Come see us at
New York Premium Incentive
Show Booth # 1230
Over 400 different companies have jumped on the phone-card train. Some are small. Some not too experienced. And many are simply middlemen with no telecommunications savvy. So who do you want behind you?
Ameritech.®
As one of the world's largest communications companies, Ameritech helps more than 13 million customers keep in touch. They were the very first major U.S. telecommunications company to pioneer pre-paid phone cards – over a decade ago. So you can truly rely on Ameritech.
And when it comes to your promotions, you can always trust Ameritech. What's behind it? Actual phone service that's friendly and efficient. Customized promotion-concept development, sophisticated market research options and a turnkey operation – all at the right price. Discover everything Ameritech can put behind your next promotion.
Call 1-888-882-2534
Ameritech
YOUR LINK TO BETTER COMMUNICATION℠
Ameritech Communications International Inc. carries calls in the areas where it is authorized. Quest Telecommunications Inc. carries all other calls.
Circle Reader No. 203
©1998 Ameritech Corporation.

Comparative advertising is sometimes hard fact, sometimes wry dismissal, sometimes ridicule. Here, a major communications company ridicules phone cards issued by unknown suppliers. Some potential users may be motivated by image, and others may be motivated by price, the weapon at hand for less well-known competitors.

or the difference between technical writers and sales writers. Transmission of information, in today's marketplace, is an imperfect competitor for effective salesmanship.

The litmus test to determine whether or not advertising has positioned a product or service uniquely might be a prospective customer's imaginary visit to the marketer in which he or she asks, "Why should I do business with you instead of your competitor?" If the answer to that question is apparent in the key lines of advertising, positioning is present; if the answer must be an elaboration of the attention-getting device in order to clarify benefit, positioning is not present.

Positioning should not happen by accident. Those who know the power of the Unique Selling Proposition reach for such a proposition not only deliberately, but sometimes painfully after much market research. Almost invariably, campaigns that last more than a few weeks are tied to positioning rather than to clever attention-getting devices.

The quandary in which many campaigns find themselves is the uneasy relationship between getting a prospect's attention in the first place and then convincing that individual or company to respond. If the prospect ignores the message, obviously that individual cannot respond. So increasingly, as advertising clutter itself increases, generating a response demands both disciplines.

A danger to which some advertisers succumb is extending their Unique Selling Proposition to the generic field of business in which they operate. Thus, a computer manufacturer may create a demand for faster computers; when the buyer comes into the store, that buyer easily can be converted to another brand. In contrast, one reason Dell Computer has dominated its field is that part of its positioning process has been elimination of retail presence. Dell does business through direct-response advertising, which eliminates the possibility of "switching" brands by a retail salesperson.

When Cyrix began producing fast computer chips, Intel, which had seen no need for an advertising campaign because buyers related the very term *computer chip* with Intel, recognized that now it faced a competitive ambience. The result was the "Intel Inside" campaign, which positioned the chip as the Rolls-Royce of chips. More valuable

Is being number two as powerful a comparative statement as being the primary supplier to a major airline? A headline emphasizing this latter point might have fewer readers wondering, "Should I look for number one?"

as a marketing weapon, manufacturers and dealers who included the Intel Inside symbol in their advertising were awarded a cooperative advertising allowance—a potent weapon in the competitive sales war. In fact, IBM, after ignoring the availability of this perk for some years, in 1997 began taking advantage of the cooperative advertising allowance its competitors had been enjoying.

Consumer demand can drive supplier demand. Until Cyrix opened the Pandora's box of competition, Intel had no need to draw attention to its product outside the orbit of original equipment manufacturers. This is not the first circumstance of its type. When aspartame—originally marketed under the brand name NutraSweet—was still protected by patent, its mere presence in the store as an alternative to saccharin-based sweeteners sufficed as a market builder, once enough advertising had convinced consumers to try it. When aspartame became available universally, NutraSweet intensified its positioning campaign by emphasizing its use in products ranging from soft drinks to yogurt, using the name NutraSweet on the product itself. Newcomers (NatraTaste) attacked the NutraSweet base through couponing in freestanding inserts, this being their own approach to positioning.

The classic example of positioning has been Bayer aspirin, which has been able to demand a premium price over other aspirins whose formulation is identical. In the field of pain relief, advertising and marketing may be at their most inventive and most competitive. Positioning often involves comparisons with other pain relievers, not just those of different formulations, but those with identical formulations. Case in point: Advil and Nuprin, whose advertising regularly attacks not only aspirin and Tylenol, but each other.

When another pain reliever, naproxen, became available as an over-the-counter item, its brand, Aleve, positioned itself as the successor to all the others. Tylenol, meanwhile, positioned itself as the principal choice of physicians. And Bayer seized the original USP concept by promoting itself as a heart attack preventive—a claim that might have been made by any aspirin, based on medical research. By saturating media with this claim, Bayer preempted competitors from sharing the benefit. Had Bayer claimed that aspirin is a heart attack

In its earliest manifestations, the Rosser Reeves Unique Selling Proposition chose elements that may not have been unique, then built a campaign suggesting uniqueness around those elements. In a contemporary incarnation, a Unique Selling Proposition uses the definite article *the* instead of the indefinite article *a* as a separator from competitors. Visualize this ad with the heading worded ". . . in the hands of *the* company. . . ." It would have hewn more closely to the USP separator concept.

preventive, benefit would have extended to all aspirins as well as to the company paying for the advertising.

The Tie Between Creativity and Salesmanship

Not until the 1960s was a major advertising agency headed by a graduate of the creative department. The creative explosion in which titans such as Bill Bernbach and Mary Wells found their names on the entranceway to the office resulted from the growing recognition that the message was as important as the medium and that without effective creative, even the most astute account management person would find his or her accounts in peril.

As seems to be true of any movement, in some cases the glorification of creative may have overextended itself. The result, some industry critics maintain, is a "creativity *über alles*" attitude in which a creative director can become a loose cannon. As one commentator put it, "These guys aren't writing copy and laying out ads. They're giving birth. They aren't creating television ads to sell something. They're creating extensions of their own egos."

How can a high-powered agency team maximize both creativity and salesmanship in the same message? Channeling creativity means putting a rein on creative directors, many of whom will object—and have on many occasions resigned rather than compromised. The logical question is, What are they compromising? An agency's function is to best represent its clients' marketing goals.

Part of the blame for any creative rebellion—if blame there be—lies in the hiring procedure in which a candidate for the two major facets of creativity—copy and art—are asked to show samples. A "standard" sample that did well in the competitive marketplace may have little glitz; a print or television ad reflecting either spectacular production or an outrageous concept may seize the eye of an agency executive looking for a new creative director, even though that campaign failed in the competitive marketplace.

Quoted in an ad for *The Wall Street Journal*, Jay Schulberg, chief creative officer of Bozell Worldwide, made this comment (on page 86):

Setting the scene with an episode that unexpectedly becomes relevant to the product is one way to break through the "clutter" of a pod of television spots. This storyboard represents such an approach. Notice the alternate endings, which those who watch televised beauty pageants will recognize as typical contestant answers.

> *There's a tendency to be blinded by flash and glitter, but the attention gained by trendy execution is, at best, a flash in the pan—and, at worst, a waste of a client's money.*

Mr. Schulberg, in a 1998 article in *Advertising Age*, pointed out that his agency had scheduled no spots in the Super Bowl telecast (thirty-second spots were selling at $1.3 million each).

An opposing view appeared in a subsequent issue of *Advertising Age's Creativity*. The editor of *Creativity*, Rogier van Bakel, wrote this:

> *Are the spots too lame for Schulberg's taste? Nope. Super Bowl commercials, the man says, are too exciting. Too entertaining.* Too popular.
> . . . *I'm with Mae West: Too much of a good thing is wonderful.* . . . *Schulberg* . . . *claims that Super Bowl costs are "an extravagant folly." They're merely forgettable "entertainment for entertainment's sake."*

The dichotomy of opinion is understandable. The editor of a publication whose title is *Creativity* would necessarily defend the creative process against a charge of "entertainment for entertainment's sake."

Rosser Reeves Lives

In his book *Reality in Advertising* (1961), the late Rosser Reeves commented on the "creativity *über alles*" syndrome. This legendary head of the Ted Bates agency wrote:

> *A man may shout from a housetop. He may blow a golden whistle and sing and dance. Because of his strange antics, people may remember what he says; but what he says may not lead them to buy.*

As described earlier, the Unique Selling Proposition, a phrase originated by Mr. Reeves, is either venerated or decried depending on an individual's position within the advertising community.

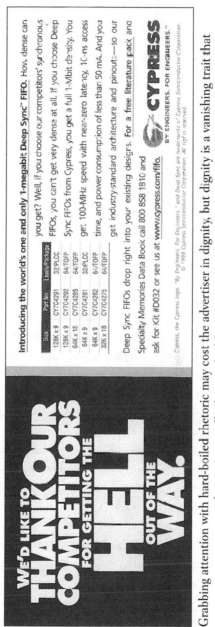
Grabbing attention with hard-boiled rhetoric may cost the advertiser in dignity, but dignity is a vanishing trait that many contemporary marketers (especially those in highly competitive industries such as electronics) regard as a liability rather than an asset.

Rance Crain, writing in the pages of *Advertising Age*, made this telling comment:

> *I've been talking to ad people who say that advertising can no longer be "linear," as it was in the days of Bill Bernbach and David Ogilvy. In other words, ads shouldn't be so presumptuous as to sell the product directly and straightforwardly. Instead, advertising's new role is to show that your product shares the same values as your target consumer. One ad guy told me his son likes the "Miller Time" ads because they're "weird," and presumably he likes the ads because he likes weird things. . . .*
>
> *Nina Cohen, the new marketing VP of Norwegian Cruise Line who just fired Goodby, Silverstein & Partners and dumped the award-winning "It's different out there" advertising, told me that the previous management at Norwegian "went hand in hand into the creative sandbox" with Goodby. Ms. Cohen said that "once you start discussing what you want, everybody at the agency was nodding their heads. But that execution was near and dear to their hearts. I can't live with it."*
>
> *Nina Cohen is my hero. She said the "It's different out there" ads were "obscure, avant-garde, slightly elitist and intimidating. People were going to their travel agents and saying, 'Put me anyplace but where I have to be naked.' Besides getting naked the ads also talked about learning a new language and making love in the afternoon and were downright 'scary' to most of the cruise line's customers."*
>
> *She acknowledged Goodby did award-winning work, but "God, isn't it over for 'award-winning work'? Somehow, it's been decided award-winning work is effective." But, she added, what Goodby did "was not relevant to our customer."*

Some thirty-six years after publication of Mr. Reeves's book, the current chairman of Bates Worldwide, Michael Bungey, redefined the term *Unique Selling Proposition*:

> *The USP is a precise term with a precise meaning. First, it is about a uniqueness that is inherent in a brand, or a claim that is not other-*

wise made in its field. It must promise a benefit that no one else is offering.

Second, a USP must sell— it must relate directly to the wants and needs of the consumer and incite action.

Third, every USP must make a proposition to the customer, a clear and compelling promise about a benefit delivered by the product. Many ads have one or two of these elements; the fusion of all three can have tremendous power.

The ultimate comment about the ongoing debate between creatives who think ads should solely be an emotional experience and marketers who want to move product may have been made by an advertising giant whose work appears in almost every anthology of great ads, William Bernbach: "Anybody in advertising who doesn't say his purpose is to sell that piece of merchandise is a phony."

Which Prediction Will Prevail?

A number of advertising executives were interviewed during the several decades before the millennium and asked their opinions of how creativity would influence the course of advertising in the years to come. Some of their comments:

Jay Chiat, Chairman, Chiat/TBWA, Los Angeles: "I see no changes in creativity itself, irrespective of the specific medium. Over 85 percent will still be mediocre. Ten percent will be inoffensive. Four percent will be interesting (perhaps even motivating), and 1 percent will be brilliant, just as it was in the sixties, seventies, eighties, and nineties."

Ron Anderson, Vice Chairman, Executive Creative Director, Bozell Kamstra, Minneapolis: "The changing media will result in creative technique modification in many cases. However, the basic premise of selling will never change."

Ian Batey, Group Chairman, The Batey Group in Singapore: "There's a risk that technology will hijack creativity—will obscure the creative process. If you're creating a page in a newspaper, or a page on the Internet, the fundamentals of brand-building still apply. You're still talking to

An example of benefit—what something will do for the person who buys it—is usually a more potent positioning point than a statement of how the product works or how it is made. While getting attention is not parallel to offering a benefit, without attention an ad may never impress a benefit on the reader, viewer, or listener.

human beings. You're still working with emotional art forms. You still have to tickle toes as well as heads."

Phil Dusenberry, Chairman, BBDO Worldwide, New York: "I'd say advertising will become more visual in the years ahead. Globalization, increased media options—all these are making consumers increasingly word-weary. We're sated with language, so messages will have to be simpler. And above all, in the year 2000, even in the year 3000, one thing won't change: Marketers who couch their product messages in humor or muse, those who entertain in order to sell, they're the ones who will inherit the earth."

George J. Hill III, Chairman Emeritus, Hill Holliday, Boston: "The message will always be more important than the messenger. So while everything evolves, the principle stays the same: Find a single, compelling idea, and express it in a fresh, powerful way."

Allen Rosenshine, Chairman, CEO, BBDO Worldwide, New York: "By the year 2000, most of the advertising in the major award shows will have become totally unintelligible to everyone including the judges (but no one will notice)."

"But We've Already Done That"

Fear of repetition has caused many a successful campaign to be replaced by a nondescript campaign, long before the original concept has worn itself out.

The Campbell Soup Company abandoned its nouveau slogan "Never underestimate the power of soup" and returned to "Mmmm mmm good!" McDonald's intermittently returns to its roots, "You deserve a break today," while experimenting with less memorable slogans. Pontiac returned to its "Wide track" USP after some years of dependence on other themes.

The endurance of memorable—and salesworthy—catchphrases, such as Morton Salt's "When it rains, it pours," emphasizes the value of an identity line even when advertising budgets are small—or, perhaps, especially when advertising budgets are small.

Generations ago Plymouth ran an ad, now legendary, comparing a carefully chosen list of its benefits with "Car A" and "Car B." Today, in a wide-open market that embraces direct comparatives, such a list (as this one) names one or more competitors. Of course, the claim has to be unassailable.

Major advertisers such as those for beer and soft drinks change their themes frequently and can achieve high visibility because of the size of their budgets. Yet it surprises no one when a major advertiser resuscitates a campaign of the past.

This is not to say that older is better. The argument about the benefit of "breakthrough" creative over the benefit of traditional sell continues to rage. What could be healthier for the advertising profession than constant reminders that the basic emotional pull of advertising never changes? Only the method of delivery is ever changing.

Interview with A. Keith McCracken

Chairman and CEO, *McCracken Brooks*
Minneapolis

How does promotion fit into the advertising mix?

KEITH MCCRACKEN: There are probably many analogies that you think of that would illustrate the old line about getting a horse to water. I think the job of advertising in the story is to get the horse to water, and what the promotion does is get the horse to drink. Now, of course, great advertising could just as well complete the whole assignment, just as innovative promotion may well get that horse to come over to the water.

The 80/20 rule says that the job of advertising is to make consumers aware of the product and to understand it. What the promotion does is change behavior. It convinces someone to do something he might not otherwise have done, to do it more frequently, and to stay in the relationship. The way promotion does that is by offering the consumer either *reduced rates* or *added value*. Sales promotion is also used to convince a consumer to make a purchasing decision within the manufacturer's timeline. So instead of you deciding you want to buy an appliance sometime within the next five years, the sales promotion team wants it to happen within the next five weeks. So they create programs that will trigger that buying decision. You may have watched an advertisement for that same appliance and decided to purchase that appliance—when you are ready, sometime in the future. Promotion's job is to shorten that time period.

So advertising and promotion don't so much compete as they complement each other?

K.M.: Exactly. Depending on the product's life stage, you'll have more or less of each of those two disciplines.

Life stage is important in the mix because when a product is first launched, there's little or no awareness and little or no comprehension of that product by the target market. So consequently the belief—or the awakened ability, or the trust, or whatever you want to call it—that causes a purchase to take place needs to be put into position.

If you think for a moment about a totally new product, a concept that we don't have any predisposition about, the job of advertising is to build awareness and comprehension as to what this product or service is. What promotion does is come along in tandem and help reduce the risk (to the consumer) or facilitate the trial experience. A very simple example is having you taste a brand-new cookie in a grocery store. That's a promotional exercise.

It's as simple as that?
K.M.: I would like to say it's as simple as that. It isn't. We're only talking advertising and promotional tactics within the broader scope of marketing communications. True marketers look at the challenge and say, "Who's the target audience? Do we want to reach them through broadcast, shotgun communications, if the audience is everybody? Or are there just ten people in the country we want to reach—in which case, let's pay them a personal visit." Marketers have to decide the degree to which the target audience is reachable by one means or another (and the most affordable means, obviously, are typically the most effective). That decision will dictate the communication style, be it advertising, direct, or in-store delivery—which typically means a sales promotion solution.

The conception is that sales promotion equals point-of-sale. How has that changed?
K.M.: Well, if you think of promotional marketing as being "behavioral marketing," that is, anything to do with change in behavior, then you can broaden the scope of exposure of the discipline to the consumer. Typically a supermarket is a delayed-consumption purchase location. You buy things to take home to eat later. You broaden it to instant-consumption purchase location (convenience stores, vending machines), and then you can think of leisure consumption locations (football arenas, beaches). Any place where the consumer is put into a position to make a

decision to buy a product or to get involved with a product as part of a promotion is effective.

This all sounds like point-of-sale, but it's in a broader sense, because typically POS is associated with a retail environment. Point-of-sale is simply a "billboard" right next to the product. It's actually "point-of-*influence*" for a purchase decision. You have to be able to buy the product or rent the product for a behavioral change to take place.

Once upon a time, sales promotion was only delivered at point of sale. These days, you may well see the promotion on a television commercial or a radio commercial. In this case you're talking about what traditionally is considered an advertising format, but it's not an advertisement, it's a promotion—or, as we call it, a promotional advertisement. And it is, in fact, a promotion, which causes you to say, "I'm going to buy two of those today because I can get some," or, "I'm going to buy two of those today because it's now a bigger box," or, "I'm going to buy two of those today because it has Michael Jordan's picture on the side," or whatever it may be that enhances the product.

What is your favorite advertising promotion of the moment?
K.M.: It's not one that's running right now, but I think one of the most impressive promotional ads I've seen in the last twelve months was the "Read Me a Story" campaign. It was a cause-related promotion put together for Visa. It enabled consumers, by making a transaction with their Visa card, to directly donate funds to a reading program aimed at children needing aid in reading, supporting the "Reading Is Fundamental" program.

This was a campaign that added value to a transaction, rather than discounting. As a result, it enhanced and built that brand's image in the eyes of a target audience while doing a service for underprivileged kids. It was effective in two ways: (1) It was clear differentiation. It was an effective way of reinforcing Visa's image, particularly since American Express had tried to stake out cause-related marketing as theirs; and (2) It was a unifying program for the card issuers and the card executors (the retailers), since card transactions were up.

Might you have approached this in other ways?
K.M.: Sales promotion can take a lot of forms, obviously, depending on the objectives and the target audience. The Visa campaign could have just as easily been "Win a trip to Disneyland." But winning a trip to Dis-

neyland is the type of promotion you would offer young families to encourage their participation in a product or service that's aimed at young kids. It's more relevant to that target audience. In this case, kids are the beneficiaries, not the target. Visa chose cause marketing to drive cash transactions and to win the hearts and minds of adult consumers who typically carry more than one credit card.

Cause marketing has its place. When it's abused or poorly used, it's very ineffective. Consumers are smarter and getting smarter, and they see legitimate programs versus those that are just borrowing the cause to feel or look good.

The other reason the Visa campaign was so effective was that every time you used your card, you were rewarded, or you actually rewarded the recipients of the program. A chance to win something can have less impact because reward is delayed. Promotion marketing splits into two kinds: immediate reward and delayed reward, which splits again into definite reward and a chance of reward. As you can imagine, an immediate discount, something free—or, in this case, a guaranteed donation to a cause—is the most impactful type of promotion, as opposed to a chance to win something later (such as a trip to Disneyland, which you don't hear about for six months).

Promotion, then, can be a stimulant?
K.M.: Of course. Promotion is often used as a tiebreaker or as a way of convincing someone to buy incremental, or more than one, product. As we examine just what initiative will get the job done, we have, through research, been able to compare benchmark promotions against historical programs on the brand or similar brands, to engage the potential consumer involvement. Now, it's a fact of life, if you talk about immediate or delayed reward in one instance and a chance or guaranteed reward in another, then clearly an immediate guarantee is more likely to get a consumer to do something he or she wouldn't otherwise ordinarily do, than a chance of winning something "one day." Upstage from this would be an "instant win" where you know today whether you've won or not. So a scratch-off game card works pretty well and is definitely better than a mail-in sweepstakes. But if I say to you, "I'd like you to buy a pack of six audiotapes, and if you do, you'll get a seventh free, or you'll get a MovieCash or MusicCash check," or some other immediate

reward, that's most likely to cause the consumer to do what you want them to do, as long as your message fits the target audience. The trouble is, of course, you can't always afford to give away a reward, so it's also a matter of budget.

Your Pete's Brewing Company promotion did well, didn't it?
K.M.: Yes, very well. When we first started work for Pete's some years ago, they were literally a small microbrewery that neither could afford nor had the distribution for advertising. So what they had to do was build the business slowly. They did it through point-of-sale. In that case, we're talking about immediate consumption on-premises, or in bars, and off-premises, which were supermarkets and liquor stores. But when you're a microbrewer, not only do you not have the national sales force, but you don't have the clout to get the retail floor space—unless you can create innovative point-of-sale that is so unique that the retailer wants to put it up anyway.

So you literally built a brand through sales promotion?
K.M.: We created equity-building programs that always had as part of them a structure that demanded floor space way beyond brand share. And as a result, we got way beyond our share of sales, and we started to catch up. So although there has been radio advertising and, for a very short time, television advertising, the brand was built on sales promotion and continues to be.

Typically, how do advertising and sales promotion split a marketing budget?
K.M.: In figuring a promotional budget in a category like packaged goods, the marketing budget is roughly split 50 percent trade promotion, and then about 25 percent consumer advertising and 25 percent consumer promotion. The trade promotion budget is an enormous part of the entire budget. It consists essentially of all those programs that are "deals" and "discounts" and anything that will drive volume directly to retailers. The other part of the budget is, typically, 25 percent of the total for consumer promotions.

Can you always get floor space in retail locations?
K.M.: The area of point-of-sale materials is actually shrinking. Because as retailers have become more competitive and have become conscious of their need to be considered "brands," they can no longer consider

Commanding shelf space in retail outlets is increasingly difficult for a new or smaller product to achieve. This innovative display for Pete's Wicked Ale created its own shelf space.

themselves a room where manufacturers put up their point-of-sale materials. They now demand custom materials or even prohibit any kind of point-of-sale materials altogether. Their reasoning: If you have two supermarkets, and they both display Procter & Gamble POS, Coca-Cola POS, and Miller Lite POS, they end up looking the same inside.

So what we're seeing is a retail branding process. And that process is driving the look that's delivered by the retailers as opposed to the manufacturer. Hence the growth of that trade budget. So now those funds are spent on co-marketing and television commercials produced for the retailer and the brand together. That's particularly true of grocery. It's less true of specialty retailers, such as stationery stores or electronics stores, where there's still a plethora of POS materials from the manufacturers. These stores still need POS because there is an increased need for explanation of what a product is. For instance, a Radio Shack store uses a lot of point-of-sale because it carries complicated stuff. It needs explanation. POS is performing a function, and the display often is semipermanent.

To what do you attribute increased attention to promotion as a component of the marketing totality?
K.M.: I think the reason promotion has become such a large part of the marketing mix is that it is a very legitimate way of building the brand, just as legitimate as public relations or image advertising or direct marketing. Promotions make you think differently about the brand just as much as behave differently toward it. And it's that combination—how you feel about it as well as your interaction with it—that generates loyal customers.

▪ 5 ▪

Media

The media director of the year 1901, compared with his counterpart of the previous century, had many choices: daily newspapers, weekly newspapers, and magazines.

The media director of 2001 has so many choices that without computerized assistance the job becomes guesswork. Not only have media expanded geometrically; market segments have subdivided again and again, making pinpoint targeting possible . . . and difficult.

The Historical Impact of Comparative Media

Until the mid–nineteenth century, "media" and "newspapers" were synonymous. Only in the latter half of the nineteenth century did magazines enter the mix. Media became, forever after, competitive.

In fact, the earliest agencies—Calkins & Holden and NW Ayer—began as media-buying services. (Some contemporary agencies have reverted to this single function, an indication of the truth of the cliché "What goes around comes around.")

When station KDKA Pittsburgh signed on, broadcasting the Harding-Cox election in 1920, broadcast media joined the battle. During the period between the two world wars, a number of ancillary media appeared, ranging from skywriting to matchbook covers.

This, too, was the time in which outdoor advertising became a major factor, originally with the ubiquitous twenty-four-sheet poster that inspired the famous Ogden Nash verse:

> *I think that I shall never see*
> *A billboard lovely as a tree;*
> *Indeed, unless the billboards fall*
> *I'll never see a tree at all.*

Fixed-position media, too, came of age during this period. Every streetcar, subway, and bus had signs on its side and display cards above its windows on the inside. Media departments of advertising agencies quickly annexed fixed-position media.

When television, which had been demonstrated as a viable potential medium during the 1939 New York World's Fair and then was in eclipse during World War II, became a factor in 1947, most advertising media departments quickly adapted themselves to this glamorous medium. For forty-five years afterward, agencies believed that the packet of media available to their clients was reasonably complete.

The advent of cable TV in the 1970s led by CNN, gave television a new dimension—niche marketing. For the first time, television could compete with newspapers and magazines in a significant capability: reaching specific target groups while maintaining the image of the medium itself.

In the early 1990s a curiosity called the Internet began its staggering pattern of wild growth. By 1995, alert agencies had as adjuncts media "experts" who specialized in this electronic wonderland.

Media Tactics and Strategies

One of the latter-day dangers facing an agency's ever-more-complicated media department is the selection of media based on the individual media buyer's personal background. In the early Calkins & Holden days, this problem couldn't exist. Selection took second posi-

The captain has turned off the seat belt sign and turned on the FLIGHTALK Network. Your customers have their headsets. The rest is up to you!

FLIGHTALK Network

Providing inflight audio and video programming for business travelers on:
American • Delta • United • TWA • America West
USAirways • Northwest • Midwest Express

To tell your story and promote your products and services, contact
Elizabeth Montgomery, Executive Producer (310)579-3326, Fax (310)579-3306,
e-mail: FLIGHTALK@aol.com-Internet: http://www.flightalk.com

CURTCO
FREEDOM
PRODUCTIONS

The media explosion seems never-ending. Here is an ad for one of the newer media: in-flight audio programs through which advertisers can tell their stories to a reasonably captive audience.

tion to negotiation. More often than not, the media buyer chose the newspaper or decided not to run ads at all. So over a hundred-year span, as media have become more and more competitive with one another, they also have become more and more competitive as choices by an individual charged with the expenditure of a client's budget.

Magazine publishers regularly complain that young media buyers shift schedules into publications with which they are personally familiar, rather than into publications that more closely match target groups. Whether justified or not, the complaint represents a red flag waving over a multimedia milieu in which no individual, however experienced, can be expected to have total familiarity with the wide variety of media choices that exists today.

According to Michael Drexler, chairman of True North Media, the availability of computerized rates in some media departments has literally made it too easy to lean toward the lowest cost-per-thousand, regardless of the demographic.

The growth of media-buying services, which we'll discuss in a moment, is the natural child of media confusion. To solve this confusion, some agencies have instituted safeguards in which the media department is given, by fiat often superimposed by either a creative team or a creative execution, a limited list of media to consider for a specific program.

Other agencies have ongoing educational updates as a regularly scheduled part of the media activity. Representatives of individual media describe the benefits and claims they regard as pertinent, and media personnel are instructed to receive this information with a totally analytical reaction.

The most valuable media director, then, is one whose background is eclectic, not tied to television or the Internet or *Rolling Stone* magazine. As clients become increasingly self-sufficient (and skeptical), the choice of media based on familiarity rather than strategy is decidedly out of fashion.

The Creative/Media Team

The synergy between those who create a message and those who place it is sometimes spotty or nonexistent—not because those who control these two areas are in conflict, but because communication sometimes does not exist.

Is it sufficient to tell the copywriter and art director, "Prepare a full-page newspaper ad," when the media department already has determined that the ad will run in *The New York Times* or *The Wall Street Journal* or *The Arlington Heights Herald?* Within each print media group, individual publications have individual personalities. The better a creative team is able to target a specific readership, the more targeted the message becomes.

For broadcast media, the differential is even more profound. A single station can represent, over a period of twenty-four hours, half a dozen separate demographic targets. So the medium becomes more parallel to the message as the partnership between creative team and media team strengthens.

In the late 1970s, the appearance of media-buying services, which offered one specialty—negotiations for advertising space and time, without the sometimes unwanted creative/production capability—prompted many agencies to unbundle media buying from their standard "mix." This enabled a former media department to become an independent competitor against the media-buying services . . . with an additional benefit: The rest of the "team" was there, if desired.

The very word *team* suggests the presence of both media and creative departments at crucial client meetings. It also suggests that the "ivory tower" isolation chosen and favored by many introverted and self-centered copywriters and artists is an ill-founded concept. The writer who moves outside his or her personal media choices should absolutely study the assigned media—and do so without a jaundiced eye.

Obviously, time spent in media study has to be figured into the total budgetary mix, but this is true whether the agency handles the media or not. The exquisite matchup of message to target is the key to rapport with the targets, no matter who has chosen the media.

Should Creativity Drive Media Selection?

Only in the post-1990 period has media selection achieved equivalence with message creation in the minds of both advertisers and their agencies. We haven't had "media heroes" until the last couple of years, and now they're featured once a month in the pages and supplements of *Advertising Age.*

The importance of media has never been questioned. What has emerged in the complex and competitive Internet-era media ambience is recognition that proper media selection can make a far more profound difference in marketing revenues than brilliant creative. (Direct marketers long have preached that proper list selection—lists being equivalent to media in this discipline—is far more likely to have a positive impact on the sale than carefully polished prose and beautiful illustrations.)

What was once a "throwaway" department, copying rates from the *Standard Rate and Data Service* (SRDS) books, has become a specialty whose top practitioners truly have achieved star value. Agencies, tiring of losing the plum billing to upstart media services, have absorbed some of these companies and/or started their own, outside the orbit of their regular office procedures.

More than any other factor, media services have contributed to the decline of the 15 percent formula for agency compensation. A major advertiser who splits assignments—creative and production to the agency, media buying to a service that specializes in analyzing and destroying rate cards—typically will pay the media service 4 percent to 6 percent. Using the traditional 15 percent formula, the agency of record would then command 9 percent to 11 percent.

Usually, though, it doesn't work out that way. Even before the rise of media services, some of the prescient had already begun to negotiate with clients on a fee basis, avoiding the 15 percent factor altogether. The original intention seems to have been the reverse of what has actually evolved. Agencies complained that they could not survive on a 15 percent level. Yet, today, few accounts are compensating agencies to that extent. (The backlash: Clients now complain that agencies are understaffed and service just isn't what it used to be.)

Evaluating Media

One reason a number of marketers have switched their media buying to media services, from the traditional posture in which the agency of

Each medium has identifiable demographics justifying the placement of advertising by those who want their message noticed by the specific target group those demographics represent. This ad isn't for the *SkyMall* publication but for a list of buyers from that publication. Mailers note parallels between the list and their own customers; based on those factors, they decide whether to rent the list.

record controls both creative and media, is a simple economic decision: The percentile cost is substantially less.

Writing in *Advertising Age* in early 1997, Walter Staab, chairman of SFM Media Corporation, made a prediction: "By the time the ball drops in Times Square welcoming in the year 2000, megasources, including mergers involving major independents, will handle as much as 75 percent of all media buying."

This vocal representative of media-buying services further predicted, "Many other agencies, large and small, will simply be out of the media buying business altogether, having transferred the media buying function to specialists."

Michael Drexler is of a different opinion. His position is that although it was predicted that media-buying services would obsolete agency media-buying departments, this not only never happened but will not happen. "Western International Media, the only possible media-buying player, never gave agency media-buying services competition until they were acquired by Interpublic."

Unquestionably, advertising agencies cannot compete in the twenty-first century unless their media buying reflects total knowledge of each medium, what the actual "reach" of each one is, and how much of the promotional information is valid as opposed to hype.

The Danger of Personal Choice

Speaking at the 1997 meeting of the European Association of Advertising Agencies (as reported in *Advertising Age*), Niall FitzGerald, chairman of Unilever and a logical spokesman because of his company's $6.5 billion annual marketing budget, made a chilling comment: "I do not find today's advertising agencies being much of a match for tomorrow's opportunities."

Mr. FitzGerald's key point seemed to be that agencies tend to use media they understand and with which they are comfortable, rather than thinking in terms of what will cause the consumer to respond. Said this powerful advertiser, "Competence in television is no longer enough." He concluded by pointing out an "alarming discrepancy between what our brands are going to need and what contemporary agencies are good at."

Should agencies regard this as an alarm call? Probably, since the giants set the trends.

Choosing the Most Efficient Medium

The most efficient medium isn't necessarily the one that will, under "laboratory conditions," produce the most results. That's because laboratory conditions tend to ignore a major factor that should be the first or second element in choosing where and how to run advertising: *budget.*

Gaining dominance in awareness, if this is the only goal, is a matter of spending the most money. Even as you see these words, you certainly sense the incompleteness of gaining dominance in awareness as the goal of advertising and marketing. The throttle needs a governor. That governor is selection of media that result in response—not just raw response from everyone out there, but usable response from the most people who can and will buy what you have to sell.

This leads us to yet another factor—efficiency of a medium in delivering those wanted consumers. Efficiency includes the three "graphics": demographics, psychographics, and geographics. This is especially valid for businesses that draw their customer or client core from a specific or limited trading area.

Implementing Media Objectives

The classic media imperative parallels the cliché describing advice to tyro stock market investors: "Buy low, sell high."

For several decades whatever heroism was allocated to media buyers centered on the ability to slash rates below the point of anybody else's negotiation. The closer a buyer could force a contract toward the zero point, the more ammunition the media department or service had in weaning business away from competitive sources.

Unrealistic? Not at all. A principal buying function is to be a consummate negotiator. But history has begun to prove that discount buying, however valuable to the profit/loss equation, is no more the alpha and omega of media buying than buying the cheapest suit from the discount store would be the alpha and omega of sartorial splendor.

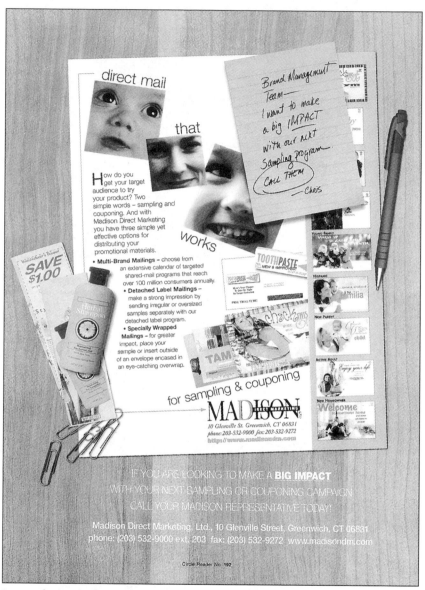

Is sampling a medium? Certainly the manufacturers of many home products use sampling as an effective way to introduce an item and give it name recognition.

Return on investment has become a more sophisticated factor as the size of budgets and arrival of new media have accelerated. Today's media buyer no longer can depend on television as the nucleus of a campaign. Not only is television itself fragmented, but buying dominance is far beyond the dollar availability of all but a handful of marketers.

For example, in 1997 McDonald's was second only to Chevrolet in total advertising expenditure, with a budget of just under $300 million. Burger King spent slightly more than $200 million, and Wendy's spent $82 million. With the three top-budgeted fast-food chains spending some $600 million, did they eliminate from the arena lesser spenders such as Kentucky Fried Chicken, Taco Bell, and Arby's? Bulk advertising can and does coexist not only with niche marketing but with targeted marketing. And the ability to juggle budgets of all sizes is one criterion of media-buying professionalism.

The Advantage of Targeting

Most media buyers would consider automobiles as a product to be mass-marketed. This position is certainly valid for many brands. But when Saab planned the United States introduction of its 1999 model 9-5 sedan, it allocated a substantial portion of its $55 million budget to direct marketing.

This component involved mailing 300,000 direct-mail packages to owners of automobiles Saab regarded as competitive, such as Audi, BMW, Infiniti, Lexus, and Volvo. Also included were existing Saab owners. The campaign included four separate mailings, offering a test-drive incentive. The manager of promotional marketing at Saab commented about this program, which was launched outside the manufacturer's normal media advertising program: "A key part of this is it's interactive. We'll seek out information and see what people's interests are and supply them with customized responses."

From an advertiser's point of view, fragmentation is both a blessing and a curse. The advertiser who wants to reach senior citizens or parents of very young children or working women has a reasonably easy time choosing media. But the recognition that reaching these

The ability of an advertising medium to attract advertisers parallels the ability of a product in the consumer or business marketplace to position itself. Uniqueness of coverage, plus buying power by those who receive it, are the keys to attracting advertisers. This publication positions itself as a high-upscale medium, whose readers have the power to respond to offers for expensive merchandise. This eliminates prospective advertisers whose wares won't appeal to the top level and attracts those whose wares do appeal to the top level.

markets requires adaptations of the advertising message sometimes limits actual participation in media reaching these groups, either because the campaign is set in cement or because the advertiser feels that targeting these groups will bleed budget away from the broader market.

The Rise of Ethnic Advertising

In almost total eclipse from the end of World War II through the mid-1970s, ethnic advertising was reborn in controversy and exists with great power, still in controversy.

No political candidate in an unmelted melting pot would risk the criticism of failing to provide a substantial part of the advertising budget to agencies that specialize in reaching black and Hispanic voters. No cable company in major metropolitan markets such as New York, Los Angeles, or Miami would dare eliminate channels whose aim is solidly ethnic. Marketers of beer, athletic footwear, and automobiles regularly allocate budget to ethnic agencies for placement in ethnic media.

Some industry analysts regard an ethnic agency's demand for a piece of the business as mild extortion, pointing to R. J. Reynolds's introduction of a cigarette that black activists claim was designed solely for black smokers, pronouncing their complaints so publicly that the company withdrew the product. Yet, these analysts point out, black agencies that militate for separate campaigns claim it is perfectly logical to mount a specific campaign for beer and spirits appealing directly and solely to black consumers.

Does appealing to a racial or religious group differ from appealing to other vertical markets such as college students or children? No one entered an objection to the "MasterCard Barbie" doll, admittedly an attempt to predispose girls to the card when they reach "credit card age." But when Stroh Brewery Company ran an ad for Schlitz Malt Liquor during an airing on MTV of a program titled *My So-Called Life*, activists objected that the program was squarely aimed at teenage girls. The Federal Trade Commission instituted an inquiry, resulting in beer companies (Anheuser-Busch and Miller as well as Stroh) canceling MTV schedules.

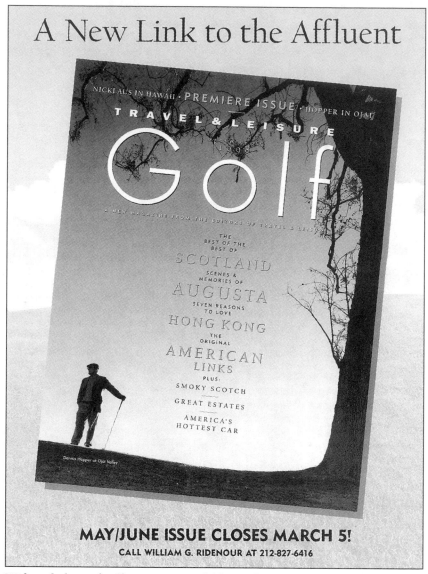

With a plethora of golf magazines available to advertisers, each must carve a distinctive editorial niche to attract advertisers. The key word in this trade ad is *affluent*.

The media logic is unassailable: The astute marketer reaches a target group as specifically as possible, provided the cost does not exceed the out-of-pocket cost of reaching that same group through mass media. National advertisers have for decades included college newspapers on their schedules. Web sites, from their inception, have boasted of their ability to penetrate vertical groups (examples: www.parentsplace.com to reach parents, www.womensforum.com to reach women).

A more psychologically based question is whether or not members of minority groups *prefer* to be reached as minorities. Or are their comfort levels and their receptivity increased when they are reached as part of the total population? Unsurprisingly, opinions are split.

Advocates of ethnic advertising say, quite rightly, that they reach their market on its own terms. In Appendix A, Stedman Graham makes a compelling case for targeting advertising to African Americans.

Advocates of mass marketing say, quite rightly, that unless an appeal is so specific that those outside a group will feel uncomfortable being exposed to it, the laws of economics suggest that a lower CPM (provided the message reaches potential buyers) should override the desire of an ethnic agency to increase its billings and the desire of an ethnic medium to increase its number of ad slots.

Nothing in the trade ad for *Heart & Soul,* a magazine aimed at black women, refers to race. Thus, the magazine positions itself as a mass medium whose vertical readership makes it a more selective buy.

A special report in *Advertising Age* in late 1997 quoted statistics from the University of Georgia and the research company Market Segment Research & Consulting. The study showed that 13 percent of the U.S. population are African American, 11 percent are Hispanic, 3 percent are Asian American, 72 percent are non-Hispanic whites, and the remaining 1 percent include American Indians, Eskimos, and Aleuts.

Certainly a homogeneous group totaling 10 percent or more of the marketplace represents a target worth approaching on its own level. In the postmillennial, multifaceted media jungle, the question of homogeneity comes into play. This emphasizes the need for both dispassionate research and specialized backgrounds within agencies catering to individual segments. For example, can a single approach

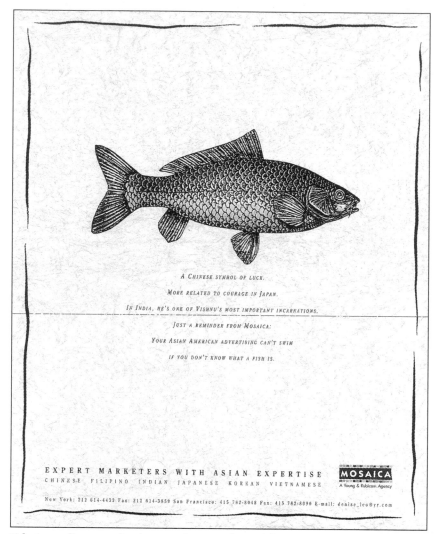

A CHINESE SYMBOL OF LUCK.

MORE RELATED TO COURAGE IN JAPAN.

IN INDIA, HE'S ONE OF VISHNU'S MOST IMPORTANT INCARNATIONS.

JUST A REMINDER FROM MOSAICA:

YOUR ASIAN AMERICAN ADVERTISING CAN'T SWIM

IF YOU DON'T KNOW WHAT A FISH IS.

EXPERT MARKETERS WITH ASIAN EXPERTISE

CHINESE FILIPINO INDIAN JAPANESE KOREAN VIETNAMESE

MOSAICA
A Young & Rubicam Agency

New York: 212 614-4432 Fax: 212 614-3859 San Francisco: 415 782-8048 Fax: 415 782-8090 E-mail: denise_leo@yr.com

Ethnic media seemed to be on a downward spiral from the end of World War II through the early 1970s. Renewed ethnic pride and awareness initiated a surge of such media, and today ethnic media and ethnic agencies are standard inclusions in most major marketing plans. This trade ad is by a company that specializes in advertising to the Asian-American market.

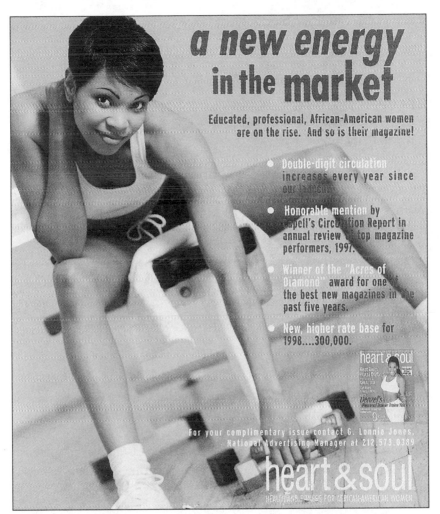

Stedman Graham points out that African Americans are the largest single minority group. This publication positions itself as a vehicle for upscale African-American women.

cover all the Asian-American groups—Chinese, Japanese, and Korean? And the Hispanic market, which ranges from Mexican and Central/South American to Cuban and Puerto Rican, is often aggressively fragmented.

Major advertisers such as AT&T have separate agencies for general, African-American, Hispanic, and Asian markets. Marketers with much smaller budgets may find the economics of minority marketing to be too formidable.

Buying TV Time

National Network Buys

A typical example of advertising in trade publications designed to attract the attention (and the schedule) of media planners is the print ad by the NBC television network for *nbc Nightly News*. Its primary selling ammunition is in its subhead: "The Largest Adult 25–54 Audience. Continued Growth. Upscale Strength."

Prime-time television is, quite logically, an appeal not only to the largest audience segment but also to the largest cadre of media buyers. One reason is that media buyers, especially those whose backgrounds do not extend to media beyond traditional mass media, may not be as adept in niche marketing as they are in estimating the cost per thousand (CPM).

The result is that when a campaign aims either its primary thrust or its secondary arm at a niche market, the advertiser might either assign that segment to a "specialty shop" or handle the marketing outside the conventional agency/client relationship. In fact, the growth of ethnic agencies seems to have been tied in direct ratio to an increase of mass-marketing-oriented media buyers within the conventional agency structures.

For nearly half a century, network television has absorbed the biggest portion of major consumer marketers' media budgets. One of the most respected media experts, Paul Schulman, of the former agency Wells BDDP, is quoted as saying, "You can talk all you want about network erosion, but people are still most interested in network TV. Everybody loves the medium."

Another expert, Stacey Lippman, of Chiat/TBWA, has disclosed his philosophy for a client with "a big problem and a small budget." Mr. Lippman chooses a quality versus quantity buying strategy, saying that such a client should prefer a limited number of high-quality broadcasts as opposed to a greater number of low-rated spots.

This classic media ad exploits the comparative position of this newscast against other network newscasts. It reinforces its argument with statistical evidence.

One of the turn-of-the-century buzzwords *reach optimizers* (analysis of a variety of television components including individual programs, individual cable networks, and individual "day parts" to put together an optimum combination of time-buys based on reach and media efficiency) is somewhat controversial. Mike Kassan of Western International Media is quoted as saying,

> *Optimization is interesting, but it's "cocktail party" interesting. Optimization is about where the industry was, not where the industry is going. While it may have great applicability in Europe, my opinion is that it doesn't have anywhere near that applicability here.*

Arnie Semsky, BBDO Worldwide's media director, takes a more cautious view of optimization calling it "helpful" but adding, "I don't think it's the end-all, be-all."

Disagreeing with these opinions, Michael Drexler opines it appears that reach optimizers are in fact becoming an essential tool for media evaluation because of the proliferation of television media choice.

Depending on the time of year, broadcast stations and cable networks are either sold out, comfortable, or sagging with unsold time. Media-buying services have centered on television as the primary source of business; the business awarded to them, in turn, has been heavily weighted in telecast media. An advantage claimed by media-buying services is knowledge of how firm or flexible television rate cards are at any particular time of year.

As is true in any business relationships, those who control the greatest amount of buying power have the greatest amount of clout with those from whom they buy. A thirty-second commercial on the 1998 Super Bowl telecast "averaged" $1.3 million. The word *averaged* indicates that some advertisers paid more and some paid less. If the differential were due only to the number of spots an advertiser bought, the playing field would be level. Was this, in fact, the sole criterion of cost? If so, no individual negotiator had an advantage. If not, the number of dollars was significant enough to cause some advertisers to question the buying power of their chosen representatives.

What about availability of openings for spots on the game as early time reservers changed their plans? The media departments and ser vices with the most intensive connections would get first choice.

The $1.3 million average was by no means the ceiling. The 1998 Super Bowl was the last under a four-year TV rights contract. Negoti- ations indicated a steep increase, which would result in a correspond- ing steep increase in spot rates. The Super Bowl long since has reached a point at which a spot *as a spot* was a questionable buy; pro- motions and tie-ins would add logic to the price.

With a handful of exceptions, such as *The Hallmark Playhouse,* total individual sponsorship of television programs is a thing of the past. (Actually, with other advertisers being allocated spots at station breaks, *no* total sponsorship exists insofar as the term implies 100 percent dominance of commercial messages during the program.) National buys are the most internally efficient and corporately prof- itable area of media activity. They require sophisticated negotiating knowledge not only of what the cost per viewer should be but also how to structure the buy so the advertiser is not "trapped" in a dead show nor forced into a higher premium for an unexpected hit show.

Spot Buys

Most independent media-buying services are more well versed in spot buys than in national network buying. The largest television adver- tiser, Procter & Gamble, sent a memo to its agencies outlining its media-buying philosophy for the 1998–1999 broadcast year. Signed by the vice president of media and programming, this memo said,

> A *new kind of planning/scheduling competency will be required to evaluate "single time" buying/information to achieve maximum results for each brand. . . . Buyers will not only be responsible for negotiating the lowest possible rates, but also for working in concert with the planning team to find the optimal buying solutions.*

A truism? Isn't negotiating the lowest possible rates and finding the optimal buying solutions the core of competence in media buying?

That the nation's biggest advertiser found it necessary to codify intended procedures in a blueprint memo indicates that media buyers have, on occasion, strayed from this chosen course.

In defense of such practices: Speculative media buying (such as placing spots in programs other than those known to be viewed by primary targets) can be the source of hidden gold, where established media buying holds few surprises.

During the previous year (1997–1998), Procter & Gamble had scheduled 600,000 thirty-second spots on local TV stations, 470,000 on national cable networks, 20,000 spots in syndication, 23,000 spots on daytime television networks, and 2,000 spots on prime-time television. One can easily see the diversity of attention necessary, comparing 600,000 local spots with 2,000 prime-time network spots. A single network spot (for example, one in the Super Bowl) can represent as much gross income as 1,000 individual spot buys. But on a net income basis, a single network spot can represent more income than 2,000 to 5,000 because of the amount of time, checking, trafficking, and administration involved with each broadcast.

How About Cable?

For years analysts have been predicting the gradual demise of network television because of the rise in cable availabilities. Yet, as cable surged, three new noncable networks, Fox, UPN, and WB, appeared and quickly assumed a competitive position. What cable channels added to the mix, aside from greater availability of choice, has been a massive group of niche markets, many with flexible rate cards. Such outlets as The Family Channel, Arts & Entertainment, and The Weather Channel—which have broad multidemographic viewership—carry heavy commercial schedules paralleling the same advertiser's scheduled on conventional television stations. Specialty cable networks, such as ESPN and Nickelodeon, offer the advertiser an opportunity to reach a vertical marketplace that combines the glamor of television with a cost structure many advertisers regard as favorable when compared with broadcast stations.

With each passing season, the total percentage of viewership on networks diminishes and total percentages on cable increase. But rates are not necessarily geared to totality, and this, as much as any other evidence, indicates the need for professionalism in media buying.

Direct-Response Television (DRTV)

Is direct-response television different from image advertising? The jury is still out. Some of the biggest advertisers claim the direct-response mantle by virtue of placing a toll-free number at the end of the spot. Technically, such a spot does qualify as direct response because of the classic delineation of the direct-response genre:

> A *direct-response message is one that causes the reader, viewer, or listener to perform a positive act as the direct result of having been exposed to that message.*

Until the late 1970s, the direct-response television advertiser had a reasonably standard marketing path. A commercial would be filmed in three lengths: 120 seconds, 90 seconds, and 60 seconds. To test the market, the advertiser would buy 120-second spots, under the logical assumption that if a direct commercial performed satisfactorily in the longer length, it would be worth trying in the shorter length; but if the campaign began with a shorter length, insufficient response would be no criterion of what might have happened had a more substantial exposition been aired.

By the mid-1980s the 120-second length had dried up, and the 90-second length was becoming available only infrequently. To those who recognized the nature of direct response—initiating an immediate positive action—lack of longer availabilities drove some campaigns into other media. Direct-response television at the turn of the century represents only a fragment of the totality of television buys. The amount is sometimes overstated by those who include as direct-response television any commercial ending with a toll-free telephone number.

Infomercials, on the other hand, seem to have increased in number—and, in fact, have attracted advertisers whose interests do not lie in generating an immediate sale (for example, automobile manufacturers). One major problem infomercials face is the limited amount of time available (primarily on cable channels and low-rated time periods). TBS Superstation, Time Warner's cable channel, discontinued all infomercial programming January 1, 1998. A spokesperson for the channel explained that this was a programming decision, not one of weak sales. At the time TBS's infomercial income was estimated at $16 million a year.

The major players in the infomercial market, such as Guthy-Renker, Hawthorne Direct, American Marketing Systems, Western International, Williams Worldwide, and WNR Direct Response, seem to agree that of ten products or services given infomercial exposure, eight will fail. For example, a company called PreventCo Inc. launched a half-hour program selling a $199 Drug Free Family Pak, using a "documercial" called "Help Your Kids." Although the kits were heavily publicized and endorsed by many experts, the program failed to sell the kits and was stopped after a two-week test. Donna Rude, supervisor of client services for Williams Worldwide, made this telling comment: "Part of the success of an infomercial lies in its wide appeal. No amount of money, media time, or tantalizing offer can overcome the problem of a product's wide appeal."

Many veteran infomercial producers share one major belief: For an infomercial to succeed, it has to be loaded with credible testimonials. No amount of demonstration can compete with testimonials in generating viewer action.

Writing in *drtv News,* Thomas Kelly, CEO of Hawthorne Direct, commented that the long-form (infomercial) marketplace seems to be shrinking, with higher rates for fewer availabilities. Compounding the reach problem for infomercial producers is fragmentation resulting from the constantly increasing number of channels from which viewers can choose. The solution, according to Mr. Kelly, is "purchasing media in larger packages or cherry-picking the best avails whenever possible." More sanguine practitioners point out that this approach is generic to discount buys. Doug Garnett of TV Tyee said, "Everybody has a rate card, but direct response is based on your ability to negotiate off the rate card."

With an exploding universe of cable channels, availabilities for long-form DRTV seem to be outside the arena of endangered species, at least for the foreseeable future. But unquestionably, shrewd media buying pertains to direct-response television more than it does to most other areas of media buying.

Magazines

Are magazine rate cards in a shambles? It depends on whom you ask.

Large buyers of space regularly buy at well below the published rate. One-time buyers regularly face the answer "Check *srds* for our rates." No surprises there. ("Remnants" are discussed later in this chapter.)

Steven Florio, president of Condé Nast Publications, has been quoted in the trade newsletter *min:* "The industry has gone backward, in my opinion. It's become something of a free-for-all."

As database sophistication moves the twenty-first century more and more away from mass targets, toward selective targets, the cost-per-thousand formula has become weaker and weaker. This has made possible the emergence of niche magazines, some of which survive nicely, and some of which—covering Internet commerce, for example—are unable to attract sufficient readership and/or advertising to justify continuing existence.

The bandwagon effect is a traditional magazine experience. A publication finds a substantial, ongoing, advertiser-attracting readership. Others follow, diluting the mixture. An advertiser whose budget is maximized either splits that budget among the competitors or chooses one or two. The Darwinian concept of "survival of the fittest" ensues, and the principal survivor is not necessarily the original publication.

An example of consolidation is Curtco Freedom Group's acquisition of *Home Office Computing* from Scholastic and merging it with *Co.,* which in turn was scheduled to be merged into *Small Business Computing.* This crowded field also included *Entrepreneur's Home Office, Working at Home, Your Company,* and *Income Opportunities.*

A circumstance a circulation manager of the 1970s would have considered quite odd: Controlled-circulation publications can have difficulty maintaining a subscriber base. Multiple mailings, E-mail,

Which way
to the gay and lesbian market?

Straight ahead.

To reach gay and lesbian consumers, a 'straight line' is not the most strategic option. Reaching this market effectively requires more than just running a few advertisements in gay and lesbian media. Like targeting any market, the key to achieving results is understanding and meeting consumers' needs.

At Significant Others, we specialise in working with clients to ensure effective brand and product positioning in this potentially lucrative segment of the Australian consumer market. Our integrated marketing services include Australia's most comprehensive gay and lesbian consumer research program, strategic marketing advice, our gay and lesbian market monitor service, specialist creative services, public relations and staff training.

To find out more about what we can do for your brand, call Ian Johnson at Significant Others. We'll set you straight.

Phone (02) 9360 2518.

Your strategic partner in
the gay and lesbian market.

Significant Others
marketing consultants

Every segment of society, whether social, racial, religious, or sexual, has its own set not only of dedicated media but of dedicated agencies and consultants. This ad, in an Australian marketing magazine, is for a company whose posture is "Your strategic partner in the gay and lesbian market."

even phone calls often fail to jog a valid subscriber into a renewal. And adding free subscribers from the "bottom"—students, those in peripheral businesses, individuals who have no control over buying within their organizations—is poor judgment.

The Circulation Race

For years *Business Week* led all consumer magazines in advertising linage. Then magazines catering to brides had a spurt. That was before mammoth books such as *Computer Shopper* and *PC Week* became such powerhouses. As this is written (early 1998), *Computer Shopper,* a monthly, had well over 9,000 annual pages of advertising, while *Business Week* had 3,885 and *Bride's Magazine* had 3,062. (After this tabulation, the February/March issue of *Bride's* carried 939 pages of advertising, an all-time high. Condé Nast claimed it was the largest consumer magazine ever printed.) Relative upstarts showed huge increases in number of advertising pages: *Travel Weekly* carried more than 5,000; and *Travel Agent* was close behind with 4,868. Among trade magazines some giants have risen: *Computer Reseller News* showed 8,186; *Electronic Engineering Times*, 6,254; *InfoWorld*, 4,188.

The relationship between number of advertising pages and gross revenues is murky—if it exists at all. *TV Guide* grossed more than $1 billion, of which slightly more than $400 million was advertising revenue. In advertising revenues alone, the leader was *People*, with $525 million—three times as much as *Computer Shopper,* despite the disparity in number of ad pages.

Parade has been the ongoing circulation leader, with more than 35 million weekly copies. But many competing publishers claim that *Parade* and its parallel, *usa Weekend,* aren't true magazines because they circulate automatically as supplements to local Sunday newspapers. Among conventionally circulated magazines, *Modern Maturity,* the publication of the American Association of Retired Persons (AARP) distributes more than 20 million copies each month. Again, competitors point out that *Modern Maturity* subscribers aren't genuine subscribers, because the magazine comes as an automatic part of AARP membership.

Who crunches 1/3 of the bars?

50+ isn't peanuts, it's 1/3 of the business in bars and just about every other consumer goods category from soup to salad dressing. If you're share shocked, it may be because you're one of too many advertisers targeting too few customers. Sweet talk 50+. Call 212·599·1880 and up your share 33%.

Modern Maturity.
A new face.
A new voice.
A new market.

The twenty-first century will witness huge growth within the fifty-plus age group. *Modern Maturity*, a publication of the American Association of Retired Persons, already has the largest circulation of any U.S. magazine—well above twenty million. Advertisers marketing insurance, vitamins, and other items regarded as competitive with those the AARP provides for its members may not have their advertising accepted by this magazine.

Millennial Slackening?

The authoritative *Capell's Circulation Report* disclosed at the beginning of 1998 that 40 percent of magazines were showing lower newsstand sales than in the previous year. Some 80 percent said direct-mail efforts to boost circulation were money losers.

Is this a trend? Veteran publishers say no trends can exist in the volatile magazine universe. They point out not only the huge list of exceptions but also the "drag down" groups, such as Internet magazines, which tended to skew total results. Further, Capell reported that half the magazines had a better pay-up rate than the previous year, while 25 percent had a poorer pay-up rate.

The most telling statistic was the overwhelming percentage of magazines whose advertising revenues increased substantially over the previous year. In contrast, revenues dropped for a relative handful.

The Post-*Post* Era

In the late 1940s, *The Saturday Evening Post,* which for decades had been the bellwether of consumer magazines and had become locked in a circulation battle with *Life,* announced that it would end the circulation race and reduce its circulation. The theory, which still holds validity more than half a century later:

> *The more promotional the effort to add subscribers, the lower the total economic base becomes. The lower the total economic base becomes, the less buying power the total circulation base has. The less buying power the total circulation base has, the less response an advertiser can expect.*

Implementing the theory was a switch from quantitative readership measurement to qualitative readership measurement. The concept, with advances and refinements, is the basis for much space-sales philosophy today.

The Magazine Publishers of America have constantly militated for more scientific readership/response measurement techniques. As a result, a principal player in readership measurement, Simmons Market Research Bureau, has refined its measurement techniques. But, as is true of all measurements of human behavior, assessing readership is an inexact science. Assessing *response* is considerably more exact, but only direct response can claim absolute measurement.

The Saturday Evening Post has been partially resuscitated but in no way reflects its former glory. Contemporaries such as *Collier's* and *Liberty* vanished in the 1950s, as television made these general-circulation magazines obsolete.

In today's marketplace, niche publications exist comfortably among the giants. *People* may be the closest to the general-interest magazines of yesterday, but for every magazine aimed at "everybody," hundreds exist aimed at "somebody." Consumer magazines edited for scuba divers, bicyclists, motorcyclists, gourmet cooks, investors, Generation X, parents and would-be parents, health and fitness buffs, owners of specific computer software, a plethora of geographic regions and ethnic and religious groups—these are a fragment of the special-interest publications destined to thrive as long as the field of interest itself and those catering to it thrives.

For many publications, advertising is as significant a spur to readership as is the editorial content. For some, such as *Hemmings Motor News,* the advertising *is* the editorial content.

Business Magazines

One of the most painful events in a business publication's history is conversion from free to paid. Some report averaging one-sixth conversion success, which results in abandoning the effort or maintaining a two-tier circulation program.

Obviously, no conversion from free to paid has ever been 100 percent successful. And, as a paid publication gains the powerful marketing ammunition "Our subscribers have paid to see our publication," it loses the competitive claim "We blanket our industry."

Successful business publications such as *Advertising Age* and *Folio* have not departed from their paid subscription base. Others, such as the dominant *Computer Reseller News, InfoWorld, PC Week,* and *Electronic Engineering Times,* achieve success through controlled saturation of their logical target universes.

Bulk is no indicator of success among business publications; rather, the key word is *penetration* within the desired core of target readers. *Hyper*-penetration within niche segments has been the guiding philosophy behind many publications. Their vertical, narrow appeal is significant to advertisers who want to avoid waste.

A generation ago, magazines edited specifically for corporate chief financial officers, credit card managers, supervisors of government travel, or users of a specific word-processing program would have been given little or no chance to flourish. Today, they not only flourish, they are like magnets, attracting competitors who salivate at the advertising in their pages.

Newspapers

When radio burst onto the scene in the 1920s, the predictions were dire: Newspapers would become obsolete in short order.

When television burst onto the scene in the late 1940s, the predictions were dire: Newspapers would become obsolete in short order.

When the World Wide Web burst onto the scene in the 1990s, the predictions were dire: Newspapers would become obsolete in short order.

Two parts of the prediction did materialize: *Afternoon* newspapers became the dinosaurs of twentieth-century communication. And "Extras" have long since vanished.

But newspapers have shown not only resilience but adaptability. Some 1,600 daily newspapers, plus more than 7,500 newspapers published on a less frequent basis, control the lion's share of local advertising.

Yes, overall literacy seems to be in a decline. Yes, the Internet has sapped reading time, as it has sapped time from all other media. Yes, it seems that every other month a crisis in the paper mills causes the cost of newsprint to rise. Yes, national advertisers and their agencies prefer the glamour, the pace, the billings, and the easy standardization of television. But newspapers continue to be the medium of choice for authoritative, dependable news in depth. Constant improvement in run-of-press (ROP) color—color throughout the paper's pages—and presswork have upped the standard halftone screen from 65-line to 85-line. Some papers can accept 100-line or even 133-line screens.

Doomsayers often overlook two natural benefits newspapers bring to the competitive arena: saturation and flexibility. Most metropolitan areas have condensed readership into a single newspaper. This makes the newspaper the only *single* medium able to achieve near-total penetration. And the advertiser can buy a one-inch ad or an eight-page spread.

Newspapers also have the benefit of short closing dates, quick substitutions, regional and/or neighborhood sections, and adjacencies to relevant editorial matter. As their emphasis has shifted from "hot" news to news in depth and features, their position in the media world seems to be reasonably secure.

For consumers, too, newspaper advertising can meet certain needs. As an old-timer put it, "They'll tear the ad out of the paper, but you won't see a customer walking into a supermarket or department store with a videotape."

As this is written, five of the ten top national advertisers in newspapers are automobile manufacturers—Ford, General Motors, Toyota, Chrysler, and Nissan. Department stores lead other categories in dollar spending.

Barter and Discount

Rate cards no longer are inviolable. One spur to the growth of media-buying services has been the constant renegotiation of rates. Obviously, though, flexibility depends on whether a market is a buyer's market or a seller's market. Too, the heavyweight advertisers are in a better position to negotiate downward from printed rates than is the occasional or small advertiser.

Barter time, which flourished in the 1960s and 1970s, has become relatively uncommon. The technique centered on a "swap" for either merchandise or programming by a supplier, who in turn would sell off the inventory of television (and sometimes radio) availabilities acquired through the barter. Beyond a given expiration date, the availabilities no longer pertained, and the amount charged from barter time was reduced as that expiration date approached.

In print media, "remnants" for magazines and "standbys" for newspapers thrive and prosper. This is especially true of national publications with regional editions. Remnants in publications, such as the weekend newspaper supplements or television program guides, invariably become available as national advertisers pick and choose based on geography or climate or individual market conditions. While this discount—as much as 40 percent off the published rate—can benefit a local or a mail-order advertiser, national advertisers cannot plan any sort of campaign around remnants, because they cannot anticipate which markets will be available.

Many newspapers—including a number that deny the availability—offer standbys. Like remnants, the discounts are substantial enough to attract mail-order advertisers, whose results have to be counted immediately against expenditure.

Those who buy remnants and standbys know the rules very well: They have hours, not days, to decide whether or not they want to buy the available space, and the ad has to be ready to go immediately.

Globalization: Will the Dream Become Reality?

For marketers who want to internationalize their message, the goal seems to be a globalization of a single message—a concept that may be legally impossible for several generations to come. Standard marketing ploys such as premiums and sweepstakes are illegal in some of the countries with the greatest buying power, Germany, for example. Comparative advertising, a staple in the United States since 1978, cannot be exported globally until some sort of international agreement makes this possible. This suggests the need for increasing sophistication within media departments to avoid last-moment rejection, which can severely damage a campaign.

The "Euro," a single currency intended as the exchange medium among thirteen to fifteen European countries, will—subject to national acceptances—immensely aid the globalization of advertising and marketing.

The Internet, which seamlessly crosses all borders, has begun a different globalizing procedure. Web sites offer a language option, payment options in multiple currencies, and quick adaptations for elements not likely to change within the first two decades of the twenty-first century—individual national idiosyncrasies and customs.

But true globalization depends less on media than on worldwide adoption of standards. Some of these standards may be less liberal than exist in individual countries, but their actuality will make it possible for the marketer to place advertising without encountering bureaucratic rejections.

The Internet as a Niche Market

The rise of the Internet as a valid advertising medium has generated the rise of specialty advertising agencies geared technically and creatively to that medium. Media buying on the Internet is more than a specialty; often it is a gamble because the World Wide Web is more fragmented than any other medium and is the least disciplined in its measurement techniques.

How does a media buyer budget for Internet exposure? Three possible procedures exist, each one subject to approval or rejection by the individual Internet search engine or service provider (such as America Online, Juno, or Yahoo!). The first, and most primitive, is simply measurement of hits on a site. For the media buyer this is the most comfortable because it most closely parallels the traditional cost per thousand. As a measurement device, it counts exposures rather than transactions, which again parallels CPM.

The second procedure measures the number of "clickthroughs" (times a user demonstrates a second-level interest by going beyond the first advertising screen). This measure counts a far more valuable target group. Obviously, charging on a per-clickthrough basis justifies a higher CPM than using the first measurement technique, just as in traditional media, targeted publications charge a higher CPM than mass publications.

The logic of clickthrough as a measurement technique was underscored in 1997, when Procter & Gamble through its agency, Grey Advertising, announced that it would buy Web ads only on a clickthrough basis. Very much annoyed, some sites denounced this policy and said they would not deal with Procter & Gamble. But once

The Internet, expected to have an estimated half billion pages by the end of 1998 and anticipating considerably more than a billion by the turn of the century, has become one of the most competitive media milieus. The purpose of this ad is to attract marketers to an E-mail source boasting (at the time) more than three million members.

major search engines (Yahoo! and Web Crawler, for example) accepted ads on these terms, a number of others made similar agreements. The logic of this procedure seems to have initiated a bandwagon effect—which, to most analysts, is a healthy move for the Internet because it ties expense to response, not to casual inquiry. Juno's advertising, directly addressed to the question of Web clickthrough, indicates marketer recognition of the difference between accidental or nonaction landing on a Web site and deliberate participation.

The third measurement technique is based on interactivity— those who have either disclosed their identity or actually entered into a transaction. Obviously, the value of such responders far exceeds that of any other groups. Obviously, too, Web sites are loath to negotiate on this basis, not only because they may feel such an agreement is a step backward toward the old per-inquiry arrangements but also because, with millions of commercial Web sites from which any visitor can choose, success on this level may depend more on support advertising in other media than on the site itself.

The ad on the page opposite is a trade ad by a company that markets audience projections for Web sites. This company says: ". . . we track users at home, business and school, and we report HHI [Household Income], age, even geographic regions. All on-line, in real time." That such a service exists is an indication of the additional information and education a media buyer should have when dealing in this exotic new medium.

The next ad on the following page offers Web sites an ABC audit. The question a marketer will inevitably ask is which of the three measurement techniques apply to any audit.

Per-Inquiry Advertising on the Web

The fourth Internet payment procedure is per-inquiry (p.i.).

The "p.i. deal" is as old as advertising itself. The very earliest advertisers made media their true partners, paying based on business resulting from the advertising.

In the 1950s, p.i. deals were omnipresent on independent radio stations. Such mail-order companies as Michigan Bulb Company

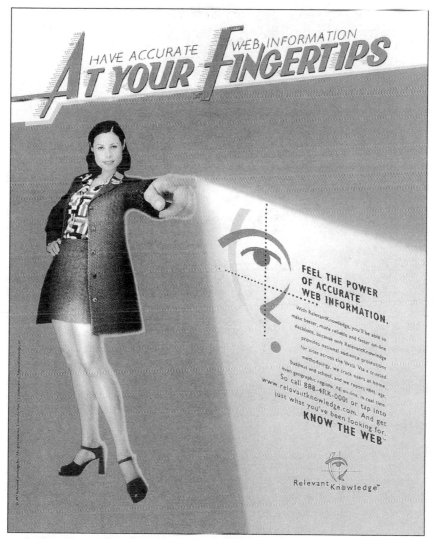

With a host of conflicting claims, any mass medium needs an outside means of determining the effectiveness of those operating within the medium. This ad offers analytical services to Web advertisers.

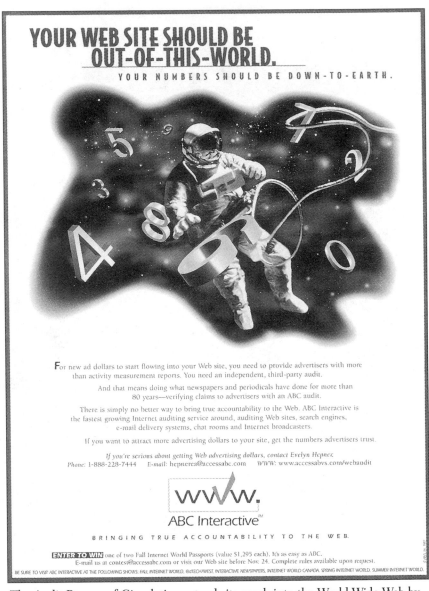

The Audit Bureau of Circulation extends its reach into the World Wide Web by offering sites hard information they can use by getting "the numbers advertisers trust."

used the technique on hundreds of stations. The most common approach was for inquiries to go to the station, which counted them and forwarded them to the advertiser, billing two to five dollars for each response. (A "response" might be a lead, or it might be a hard order.) Considerable cable business uses the per-inquiry method, although some cable systems insist on a straight time-buy before considering p.i.

In 1998, Garden State Life Insurance Company of Texas pioneered this method on the World Wide Web, paying ten dollars for each lead realized from a contracted site—Insurance News Network (www.insure.com), GolfWeb (www.golfweb.com), and DoubleClick Direct (www.doubleclick.net) were three.

Per-inquiry, once the "ghetto" of advertising, can generate income from dead radio time, from unsold print space, and from the limitless reaches of a Web site.

Which Dollars Go Where?

Advertising Age reported in late 1997 that an on-line brokerage service called Suretrade.com had launched a multimillion-dollar on-line ad campaign, in addition to advertising in conventional media such as cable TV and print. The advertiser assigned on-line advertising to one agency and off-line advertising to another agency. A consultant to the company indicated that budget would be split fifty-fifty.

Advertising in media promoted the on-line address, without which no transaction with the on-line brokerage service could be possible. The company's Internet address was on the screen throughout its thirty-second television commercials. On-line links and banners on some fifty Web sites led directly to a potential transaction, as well as offering additional information.

A major indication of the evolution of the Web as a niche market medium was the agreement between Dreamworks Pictures and Curiocity's FreeZone (an on-line structure aimed at eight- to twelve-year-olds that gets three million page views a month by juvenile site visitors) for on-line promotion of children's movies. The interactive offerings on this Web site include chat sessions with movie cast members and prizes for navigating an on-screen maze. The intention seems to be a synergy in which media advertising for these motion pictures is enhanced by generating a more intensive desire to see them, along with use of the Web site to introduce the movies so that when media advertising runs, they already are a brand name.

Implementing and underscoring the Internet's position as a labyrinth of niche markets, PointCast has become the prototypical news and information service for on-line targeted ads and news bulletins. Properly structured, the system brings to an individual computer developments in media, finance, or even straight news on a timely basis. PointCast is the first "ads on demand" procedure: Targeted advertising pops up within the individual user's own screen, determined by the type of information the user has specified he or she wants to see. The company has had, as of this writing, indications of success in selling advertising from a formal rate card.

An indication of ongoing fragmentation—which may, in fact, bring the Internet into total media-buying equivalence—is the development of specialty media services such as the Women's Forum ad network and Women's Wire. Women's Wire, even in its earliest days, attracted a roster of blue-chip advertisers such as Oldsmobile, Levi Strauss & Company, and L. L. Bean. At its origination, the Women's Forum was selling banners at a rate of $38 per thousand impressions.

Is the Internet a separate phylum, outside the arena of accepted advertising media altogether? A study by BJK&E indicated that Internet users tend to be younger, more highly educated, and have a higher household income than adults in general. This data is not surprising, nor is it intended to be a permanent analysis.

On-line media planning, which began on a helter-skelter basis, has been sophisticating itself so quickly that some of the early "Let's get on the Web" enthusiasts have been left behind. Twenty-first-century Internet media expertise will center itself on connecting people who want to find either a specific site or a specific business category. The era of mass exposure, whether that exposure reaches logical targets or not, deserves to be in eclipse.

How to Choose

Which medium is the best buy for any product or service?

The answer may be a truism: the medium that offers the best targeting at the best price.

Lowest cost per thousand is semi-obsolete; media buyers long since have recognized that the lower the CPM, the greater the amount of waste. Yet waste is often a speculation rather than a fact. Marketers, especially in mature industries, need growth, and growth comes more from the outside than from the inside.

A telling comment comes from Michael Drexler: "The changes we've seen in media in the last several decades are nothing in comparison to the metamorphosis we're going to see over the next ten years as a result of the interactive potential and measurability of the new digital frontier."

The most logical approach in the high-cost twenty-first century seems to be dedication of the greater percentage of budget to tested, targeted media, with allocation of speculative budget to outside media whose potential seems most credible.

This is the challenge that has made media buying a profession rather than a way station.

■ 6 ■

Production

With the decline of the 15 percent commission structure, advertising agencies have been witnessing a quiet rebellion by their clients against the 17.65 percent production markups that have endured for more than a century. (Much of the rebellion is self-caused: Agencies too often artificially impose markups of 50 percent or more. In some cases extra markups are justified because clients insist on multiple changes for which they won't pay. But once tarnished, the agency's image is that of a greedy leech demanding unreasonable payment for services not performed.)

The paradox of the entire relationship is that the 15 percent commission was based on a client not paying for creative work. With the commission structure in a shambles, many clients cannot see the logic of paying for what they once accepted as part of the total package. We have discussed some of the elements of this problem in the chapter on budget. This chapter deals with elements of production outside the potentially profitable arena of media placement.

Television Advertising Production

The rise of heavily produced television commercials has led many agencies to dedicate the bulk of their creative resources to the video medium. Television, with its quick "die rate" demanding constant replenishment of messages, obviously demands more attention to production than the traditional sedate print media, the production-easy radio medium, or even the still-evolving Internet.

Until the mid-1950s, local television commercials as well as many nationally shown commercials were produced on sixteen-millimeter film. Some, in fact, were simple thirty-five-millimeter slides. Commercials heavy in effects were necessarily shot with thirty-five-millimeter film because of the image deterioration, generation to generation, in the production process.

This gave rise to a two-tier production universe in which the gap between a "budget" spot and a "major-league" spot was substantial. Within this two-tier positioning, clients themselves were necessarily regarded as budget-conscious or production-prone. Agencies pitching accounts made this a major factor in their client courtships and creative proposals.

The rise of videotape leveled the playing field considerably, because so many suppliers had parallel equipment and production crews. This, in turn, gave rise to a "star system" among television directors at the various studios, who had been able to charge premium prices for the use of their name on the commercials, regardless of the content of the commercials. Some of these individuals are, in fact, primarily feature film directors. The impact of their personalities has generated an unusual question:

What Is the Agency's Role in Television Production?

In a classic circumstance, an agency's creative team presents a story-board or even rough footage to a client for approval prior to placing the commercial with a studio for actual production. (Some agencies also own and/or control the studios in which they produce most of their spots.) Once the client and agency have reached an agreement, if the commercial is to run on more than a local level, good business judgment calls for the agency to submit it to the networks in storyboard form. The purpose of this network clearance is to prevent rejection after the commercial is finished. (Example: A commercial innocently used the word *Eskimo*. A network rejected it as a pejorative term, requiring replacement with *Inuit*.)

Once approved, the commercial is in three sets of hands: the agency's, the client's, and the studio director's. The cost of production is subject to agreement by these three parties, which sometimes is difficult to achieve. A fourth set of hands sometimes intrudes—the talent, especially if the message is to be delivered by a "star."

Some clients are nonplussed by the amount of time to shoot what they regard as a simple thirty-second commercial, calculating—seemingly logically enough—how much time it should actually take to shoot the scenes in a commercial plus the number of hours in an editing control room. While their viewpoint has validity if one excludes the human factor, in actuality few television commercials can elude the problems resulting from individual viewpoints, as those viewpoints are exposed and amplified under actual battle conditions on the set. In theory, all parties in a decision-making position have the same goal; in reality, each may be self-serving—a sample for the reel, ego massage for the next higher-up on the corporate level, or a series of scenes the talent can use to show to an agent.

The question of who should have ultimate control is moot, as is always the case when one party is spending money and another party claims greater expertise. Some industry analysts claim that more accounts change hands because of disagreement as to what makes an effective television commercial (regardless of exposure to focus groups) than for any other reason.

For smaller accounts, the ratio of cost between production and money spent for media exposure is a far more significant factor than for major accounts. Advertisers with budgets running to seven or eight figures quite regularly dedicate half a million dollars or more for production of a single commercial. For the smaller advertiser, the typical production budget is seldom more than 10 percent of the total allocation for television and is often considerably less.

Television Production Technology

In its early days—through the mid-1950s—television offered limited and sometimes embarrassing options for producing commercials. The advertiser had a choice of "live" presentation, which could have bizarre results, such as the now-historically-famous sticking refrigerator door or the occasional dropped or forgotten line; slides, which although lacking in motion, were advantageous for the now-departed low-budget advertisers; or black-and-white film.

Videotape transformed commercial production as much as it did news and dramatic production. Originally, taping was on a massive Ampex two-inch recorder, which made location taping difficult. The arrival of color videotape and the high-fidelity one-inch originals made this the medium of choice for the great majority of commercial productions. U-matic ¾" tape became the standard release format.

For other than television station use, only in the last several years have videotape players incorporated the ability to reproduce both the leading standard methods—NTSC, in use in the Americas and Japan, and PAL, in all of Europe except for France. (France has its own system, SECAM; with its 825-line resolution, it was technically superior until the introduction of high-definition television.)

The Cost of Talent

One key element in television commercial production is the cost of talent. An advertiser does have a choice: members of Screen Actors Guild (SAG) or American Federation of Television and Radio Actors (AFTRA) or nonmembers. Most of the major advertising agencies have become signatories to the Screen Actors Guild agreement, which means the clients of these agencies are subject to use payments depending on frequency of broadcast and whether the commercial runs after its initial thirteen-week period.

For the national advertiser, the cost of talent may be inconsequential in an era in which total production cost may be half a million dollars, against a media budget of $10 million or more. For the smaller advertiser who may produce the commercial locally through a nonsignatory advertising agency, the universal availability of videotape facilities represents the possibility of professionally competitive results at a substantially lower cost than would be the case if production were still film-reliant.

Newspaper Advertising Production

Old-timers still remember when newspapers were printed by letterpress process. Advertisers would send their display ads in fiber-paper mats.

To prepare the mats, the advertiser or production house would set type in the classic hot-lead manner, usually using a Merganthaler Linotype machine for text and a Ludlow machine for display type. Newspapers were almost universally geared to sixty-five-line screen. The ad would include the halftones in position. The newspaper would handle the ad as it handled its own editorial matter, pouring the lead into the mat to achieve a printable plate.

Because the metal was soft, as a press run progressed the image would become increasingly less well defined. Newspapers had long since adopted the habit of sending advertisers tear sheets from the early part of the press run. In fact, while the editorial matter might be replated several times to incorporate late-breaking news, a full-page ad might continue with its original plate. This occasionally gave an edge to smaller ads, which, on the same page as editorial matter, would have a fresh image.

Rotogravure represented an escape from the low-definition letterpress method. Even as early as the 1930s, newspapers regularly carried rotogravure sections with their Sunday editions.

The IBM Composer, which became popular in the late 1960s and early 1970s, began the death knell for the Linotype machine. Hopelessly primitive by today's standards, the Composer offered kerning and a minimal choice of typefaces in sizes from six points to eighteen points. The first Composers required typing each line twice to achieve full justification. Later models improved on this by electronically noting the spacing and making the adjustment for the typist.

Today, not only is 85-line screen standard for newspapers, but some claim they can handle 100-line or even 133-line screen. Mats and letterpress have become historical oddities, and some newspapers display a Merganthaler Linotype machine as a museum piece (right alongside the Underwood typewriter).

The first truly electronic typesetting was the Compugraphic machine, which dominated type composition in the late 1970s. The Compugraphic was the precursor to desktop publishing and was the last area of dominance by typesetting houses, who either switched to Compugraphic from hot type or perished.

Today, when a single CD-ROM can have thousands of fonts and limitless availability of size from one point to six hundred points, the advertiser has no problem fitting type into an ad or choosing from an exotic selection of typefaces. Newspapers can prepare ads for local advertisers in minutes rather than days, and the concept of waiting at the Linotype machine or burning one's fingers to carry a single slug, which would replace a line that might have a misspelled word, is a concept completely unknown to today's generation of art directors.

Usa Today has revolutionized not only the approach to editorial coverage in newspapers, but also their image as an entertaining "read." When *The New York Times* in late 1997 added ROP ("run of press," which means universal availability within the newspaper's pages) color, it was a concession to the changing role of newspapers in the communications mix.

With the prevalence of ROP color, the cost differential between monochrome ads and ads using color has lessened considerably. In some sections such as the comic strips and, of course, the freestanding inserts such as Valassis and News America, color is standard and has no surcharge.

The advertiser of the twenty-first century has a huge advantage over the premillennial counterpart: color separations. Scanning has eased and automated separations so that a more typical way of sending advertising to a newspaper is either on a computer disk or directly by E-mail. The benefit extends far beyond the time and the money saved. Any advertiser who was in the marketplace as recently as the 1980s remembers getting an angry phone call from a publication, at the moment of an already extended closing date, complaining that the emulsion of the film was on the wrong side. Another benefit is not having to prepare board "mechanicals" for each newspaper, as used to be the case, in which advertisers might ask a publication to "bicycle" the board to the next publication and hope that it would not become damaged in transit.

The simplification (if electronic production can be called that) of print production methods has brought newspapers closer to magazines in print quality—and magazines closer to newspapers in closing dates.

Magazine Advertising Production

Much of the history of newspaper advertising production, especially regarding typesetting, also applies to magazines.

Magazines were early converts to offset printing, which required film instead of mats. And even half a century ago, most magazines that were printed on supercalendared paper accepted halftone screens of at least 133 lines and often 150. Publications printed on enamel stock could handle 200-line screens—still the usual maximum today.

The surcharge for magazine bleed pages has always been a chimera. To some advertisers a bleed surcharge is an outrageous scam, a bald attempt to increase revenue without accompanying benefit. To others bleed means both an extra half inch to three-quarters inch in ad height and width, and a more extravagantly dominant look to the ad itself. The argument is sometimes moot, because technological advances have made possible printing of some publications with no additional cost for bleed.

A development of the 1980s that is reaching full flower is "selective binding," in which a magazine appears to be edited and have an advertising content specifically for the recipient. The advertiser has the opportunity to split-run advertising so individual copies can be targeted to individuals who have expressed or are on record as accepting specific offers. Not only that, the ad can include the person's name within the text.

Early efforts at selective binding were, to the professional eye, obvious both in typeface and in positioning of the personalized elements. As the technique grows more sophisticated, personalization becomes both seamless and transparent. This opens avenues for hyperpersonalization such as individualized couponing, invitations, and dealer references within specific geographic areas and zip codes.

Direct-Response Production

From the period immediately following World War II to the early 1970s, direct marketing—then synonymous with direct mail—gradually declined. Suddenly, in the mid-1970s, revival occurred.

Technological advances are secondary to electronic advances in the area of direct-response advertising. Four developments have been most responsible for propelling this medium into the forefront of marketing. Two of these are the computer and postal codes, both of which have multiplied the potential for hypertargeting as database and geography marry to provide the marketer with fewer speculative targets and more prequalified targets. The other two developments are toll-free telephone numbers and universal distribution of charge cards. These have extended the capability to make ordering fast, easy, and simple.

Electronic typesetting, digital photography, and the replacement of the traditional four-color separation procedures with electronic scanning have given advertisers great latitude in the creation of direct-mail packages. Too, tests have become substantially easier to create, since changes can be made within moments.

Testing is also more valid when computerized analyses are used. The marketer can detect minuscule variations based on geography, age, gender, income, neighborhood, family, and dozens of other parameters.

List Selection

List sorts have become more and more specific. Thus, even though the raw cost of names to whom a direct mailer sends an offer has skyrocketed, the possibility of one list out of a group performing strongly has increased. So a mailer may test ten lists of 5,000 names each.

Assuming the universe of each list is big enough, if two of those lists pull well on the test, the mailer can anticipate success for the rollout.

List selection is simply an academic exercise unless one adds to it a comparative analysis of the pulling power of various lists. Thus, a crucial part of production is instruction to the lettershop (the company that addresses, inserts, and mails) to code each list, usually on the response device. Without this, no database can be complete, because the mailer is unable to determine the source of buyers.

In a classic circumstance, the value of list selection as a sibling of effective database use can be shown quickly: Suppose for example, the mailer tests 5,000 names from each of ten lists. Each list has a universe of, say, 100,000 names. From the test, the mailer learns that two lists have been profitable, two lists have performed at a breakeven rate, and six lists are "dogs." Is the mailing potentially profitable?

Remarkably so! At the very least, the mailer can anticipate a rollout of 200,000 to lists of proved effectiveness. The mailer also might analyze the two breakeven lists to see how they differ from the two lists that pulled best. With some logical tweaking, these lists can be pushed into the profit column.

This example is admittedly simplistic, but it demonstrates the importance of list selection and analysis as part of the direct-mail mix.

Mailer Variables

Other elements of production, often overlooked by noncareer direct marketers, are choice of paper, number of colors, envelope size, number of personalized elements, postage type, size restrictions, quantity, and premailing preparation to maximize postal discounts.

The mailer who produces all elements on enamel paper is not only sacrificing substance for form, but also spending money for what could be a reverse effect. The letter need not (and usually should not) appear to be heavily produced, because a heavily produced letter betrays the commercialism behind it, damaging rapport and verisimilitude. Lasered personalization works poorly on coated paper and adds expense without adding impact. When planning lasered personalization, the marketer should be positive the print buyer is familiar with the accept/reject reaction the lasering process can cause: Lasering should be done only on paper treated for lasering.

Because the typical mailing includes three to six elements, having every component in the same color can reduce the visual effectiveness of each one.

In short, this is a medium in which isolating production from the total creative/marketing planning can damage both budget and response.

Electronic On-Line Media

The key advice about production of an on-line marketing message has to be a truism: Even more than is generic to television, on-line marketing marries the creative to the technical.

Production seems to develop in two directions. Contemporary word-processing programs include HTML (Hyper-Text Markup Language), which enables anyone to prepare a basic message for a Web site. The increasing sophistication of Web sites, with motion and sound, make this approach as basic as the use of slides for television commercials. So HTML does represent the capability of getting on the Web but not of preparing a visually exciting message.

The issue of visual excitement is unresolved and may always be, just as it is in the medium of television. Highly produced Web sites have two implicit problems. First, they download slower, and second, they are much more difficult to change. Major marketers have established on-line departments staffed by technicians whose job it is to stay abreast of developing techniques and apply them to the Web site. With some sites requiring thousands of pages (for example, automobile manufacturers whose many pages change with each year's model), a complete department certainly is necessary.

One caution that might apply is the recognition of the Web as a *marketing* medium. Overdependence on technicians can result in a handsomely mounted message with little sales impact.

An often-overlooked component of on-line production is the banner. One reason it can be overlooked is that not all marketers use banners as a cross-reference to their Web site. For those who do—and on-line clutter, increasingly epidemic, makes banners more and more competitively necessary—recognition of banners as a prime referral mechanism includes recognition of the need for bright salesmanship in these miniature billboards.

Alternative Media

The category of alternative media includes widely diverse marketing tools, ranging from fixed-position signs on buses and taxis to package enclosures. The common element among them is immediate attention grabbing.

Fixed-position media have to sell at a glance, so their message cannot be complicated. If the message is necessarily complicated, the solution lies in media rather than production: Fixed position is the wrong medium. Fixed position is an ideal medium for mnemonic treatment—reinforcing a name, such as a currently released motion picture, a new product heavily advertised elsewhere, or a physical location the marketer wants known by its name.

Package enclosures, another category of alternative media, have little in common with a fixed-position sign. This is because the purpose of a package enclosure is to effect an immediate sale, demanding explanation. Package enclosures have the restriction of maximum size imposed by either the company sending the package to its customers or the broker handling the transaction. Because so many package enclosures are nested in a pod of many, an effective enclosure necessarily screams for attention and offers an easy way to order.

In the mid- to late 1990s, telephone cards have become an often-effective alternative medium. These cards, used as premiums, offer x minutes of free long-distance calling. They become an advertising medium because when the user calls the toll-free number, a recorded commercial message of five to ten seconds plays before the caller can dial the desired number. Many users of phone cards regard them as goodwill builders. This position seems logical because the caller is not thinking of responding to a commercial message but is, rather, in a positive frame of mind relative to the name of the sponsor printed on the card.

Production Logic

Relegating production to a ghetto position within an advertising agency or a marketing company can be more than a tactical mistake; it can split both responsibility and decision making, sometimes into fragments.

Production, is, after all, the final touch to both the marketing intention and the creative process implementing that intention. If the target, exposed to the result, has less than a maximized response—and that failure is because production did not match what might have been maximum reach—then what should be the final touch of professionalism has failed. This is not necessarily the fault of production people. If they lack participation in the decision-making process, they may go their own way and produce materials that are visually elegant but psychologically defective.

Production, then, is not a stand-alone. As is true of every major facet of marketing, it should be integrated into the total mixture, with its own experts watching over it—and being watched over.

Interview with Tom Veazey

President, Bucaboo Company, Glen Allen, Virginia, and former
Executive Vice President, Automated Enterprises Inc.
Ashland, Virginia

Do you see or have you seen any relationship between production of a direct-mail package and the amount of response that package generates?
TOM VEAZEY: Yes. In the last three to five years, I've seen a move toward better list selection, more refined testing processes, and a higher budget dedicated to production of the direct-mail pieces. I've seen clients mail less with a greater degree of certainty to the response they expect to generate, so they're putting more money in the production: use of more color, selection of higher-grade paper, more personalization. We're finding there is a direct relationship between results and a higher-quality produced piece.

I'm hearing it from the traditional fund-raising and nonprofit clients as well as from the financial and business-to-business arena. They're reporting they do see a relationship between production and results the direct-mail piece produces.

Are there any exceptions where people would say, "I have a finite budget, and I'm going to put x amount of money into reaching more people rather than a better quality paper or more colors"?

T.V.: I think we still see that in certain segments in the nonprofit industries. They're appealing to people to donate money to a cause that apparently is in dire need of money. The production quality of the piece matches the cause. They don't want too much glitz, which destroys the "We need the money now" image.

Also, if you're selling something at a bargain, low-price, low-ticket one-time introductory offer, the question is, Do you do a four-color brochure about this very inexpensive piece? No. You're going to have to do a one- or two-color brochure that matches. Production values need to match the product you're selling.

The financial marketplace is becoming such a major player in direct mail, and I'm seeing the financial industry putting an increasing amount of money in production to advertise high-ticket products. I've also seen circumstances where simplicity helps response, such as 8½" × 11" written letters inserted into a number 10 closed-face envelope with a first-class stamp.

The deciding factor, really, is the marriage of the creativity with production. It's essential that production becomes part of the creative process to control budget and also to control the actual manufacturing of the piece.

What is the current production state of the art?

T.V.: The current inserting machine you'll find in 80 percent of letter-shops in this country is the old six-station Phillipsberg inserter, believe it or not, with a meter head on it. They added a stream feeder to the pockets that allows us to insert the clipped-on devices and an accordion fold.

But the state-of-the-art machines today are the intelligent inserting equipment that allows you to have six, twelve, eighteen, twenty-four, thirty-six pockets, and they read bar codes on the address piece with selective insertion so that one person gets one version and another can get a completely different version based upon buying habits.

The bar code is similar to the bar code at the baggage counter in an airline terminal. For example, your American Express statement could be one page or twenty pages, and it reads the bar code on each sheet to tell how many pages should go to whom. It knows when to stop sending pages and to move on to a new statement.

The logical future would be anticipation of greater and greater ability to personalize the mailing from front to back, even to an audience of one. That audience of one in direct-mail production is the next battleground. It's the ability to, on a consumer-by-consumer basis, personalize a mail piece beyond just identifying what a credit limit is or past buying habits. It's the ability to select inserts that match a customer's specific interests. It's possible that no one person gets the same combination.

What about personalization? Is that also unlimited?
T.V.: I can't go as far as to say it's unlimited, but it's extensive, and we're personalizing multiple pieces efficiently. We now have more and more connectivity between equipment, enabling us to take ink-jet, laser, web printing, and folding equipment and link it all together and do multiple hits of personalization in a package, so your reply piece, your BRE [business-reply envelope], your outside envelope, your stick-on notes, and your letter, as well as the invitation and the coupon, are all personalized.

In times past, production people have been terrified of W folds and Z folds because they would hang up the machines. Is that still a problem?
T.V.: Ask your lettershop if they have an extreme feeder. It uses friction to pass the piece into the belt opposite to the clamp and jaw device. So no matter what the fold is—anything beyond a business card–sized piece—it will go into the envelope, even if the open end goes first. It's a technology you have to have to remain competitive in this business and provide service.

Also, the cost of personalization is going down. Looking at continuous-form lasering, we're seeing that if your job is, say, 100,000 pieces or less, it didn't used to make sense to do continuous laser. Now with 5,000-, 10,000-, 15,000-piece runs, it economically makes sense to go with continuous-form. The availability and the technology have driven the cost per thousand down on these machines. Siemens fifteen-inch-wide equipment allowed you to only do fourteen-inch forms, so you could only do a two-up, monarch-size (7" × 10") form. You couldn't do a two-up, side by side 8½" × 11". The IBM 3900 Wide Web is eighteen inches wide, so you can run a two-up 8½" × 11", two 8½" × 11" or 8½" × 14", 11" × 17", or 21" letters side by side. So you're getting twice as much on the three-foot side, and you're getting two letters per inch instead of one letter.

The high-resolution "advance function" printing, which adds to the resolution quality, has made continuous lasering as attractive to the eye as the 400- and 600-resolution sheet print. We now see people doing dual-part continuous lasering. We can laser the front and the back using two machines together. We're doing roll-to-roll continuous laser, so you skip the fanfolding and pin feeding.

So we're saving money. Spot color is fairly regularly available on cut sheet in most markets and is becoming more available in continuous forms. In larger markets spot color MICR [magnetic ink character reading] is available on both cut-sheet and continuous form.

Can you explain the two terms spot color *and* MICR *encoding?*
T.V.: Spot color is the ability to add a single laser color that can be personalized for a signature, handwritten line, underscore, or logo. So in some applications, if all you have for an additional color is the logo, you digitize the logo and have it lasered onto the letter in spot color. Or if you want to send a bulk letter in which you personalize the recipient's name in handwriting and the letter is signed in that same handwriting, both in blue, and yet there's also a typed name and address, spot color lasering allows you to do it in one step.

MICR encoding allows you to laser the code in magnetic ink in an OCR [optical character readable] font such as the financial institutions are using for transaction documents. So when we do "live check" packages, we can MICR-encode the recipient's account number on that device. This process has become fairly standard.

Do you see any trends in papers or the use of papers?
T.V.: We're finding that laser refinements enable us to venture more and more into some coated stocks without smearing.

But I still don't want to do large runs with cut sheets lasered on a high gloss, because the laser image has a tendency to stand out on the surface. If it's not sealed through the laser, it can burnish off through the handling process. However, matte papers laser very well. The paper companies have changed chemical compounds to make their papers more laser-friendly. Still, extremely "toothy" paper with a lot of texture to it does not take laser well. I suggest testing it before a laser run: Have your paper house send you ten sheets of 8½" × 11", and run it through your best desktop laser printer. If it doesn't work with a good desktop printer, it probably won't laser well in a production environment either.

Super-gloss finishes are a big laser problem. We are lasering pieces that have been spot-aqueous-coated or -varnished, leaving an uncoated window area for the laser information.

The other development that's really helping the industry is high-speed, high-quality ink-jet that's got resolutions of 240 × 240 and 300 × 300 dot-per-inch ink-jet. It doesn't look like some of the old magazine ink-jet typography that tends to angle to the left or to the right. It's better quality multiple-head, where we can do a return address or recipient's address, a bar code, and even a personalized message in a high-quality ink-jet. It's very fast, and it's less expensive than lasering.

Incidentally, it's no longer necessary to laser on specific laser paper, but you still do need to preprint using laser-safe ink. Take a four-color process: Everyone is now lasering over four-color process printing, but you still need to specify laser-safe ink when you spec your printing. If a printer isn't familiar with it, find another printer. Don't let a printer become educated at your expense.

You raised the key point here. If you were to give advice to someone in the world of conventional advertising who might be considering going into direct mail without the background of production, without the background of some of the terminology, what in a couple of paragraphs would you advise that person to do?

T.V.: Find a resource in your direct-marketing community who is well versed in all aspects of direct-marketing production. Hire them on a job basis or retain them. Sometimes they'll come in and help you with it just for an opportunity to bid on it. If you're looking at agencies, find out if the agency has this capability. Do they have someone in-house who's knowledgeable in direct-mail production, or do they have some-one they use?

The process requires professional knowledge. Lasers, both continu-ous and cut-sheet, have size restrictions. Know what those size restric-tions are before you print. If your intention is to originate your own envelope or your own form, whether it's continuous or cut, or your own pieces, and supply everything, and be your own contractor, as opposed to hiring a professional, be mindful of type of paper, finish of paper, direction of the grain. For example, you can't run a 4" × 6" postcard through a laser printer, because it's too small. You have to print it two-up 8" × 12" and then cut it in half after it's lasered. You only print 5,000 sheets, get 10,000 postcards. You're only lasering 5,000 sheets, but those are little things that the printer might not know, the lettershop might not know, but your laser house would.

The production industry tends to parallel most industries. It ranges from boutique to full-service. There are lettershops that can do all of this in some markets, and other markets are still very boutique oriented. In such circumstances you'd deal individually with an envelope printer, forms printer, high-quality web printer, and laser shop. You may not have one source who can do it all, and it's very hard for one source to be all things to all people. That's why I recommend getting the services of someone who is a professional in direct-marketing production to help train all your people. The cost of using someone like that is paid for many times over.

■ 7 ■

Testing
and Research

One would think the research aspect of marketing would be one of the least controversial aspects.

Quite the contrary. Research has not fallen from its lofty pedestal but has certainly come under attack by those who point to flaws in both the method of research and the applications resulting from research.

Much of the controversy stems from the individual marketing philosophy underlying the source of a campaign. The hard-boiled, results-oriented marketer cares little for theory and motivation unless those two elements tie directly into the promise of an improved bottom line. The advertiser who separates the advertising function from the totality of marketing similarly separates transmission of image or brand from results.

Thus the quiet argument rages. Research that gears itself to the traditional terms *noted* and *recall* is of value when the advertiser's concern is number of people reached. This same approach bleeds over to Web site analyses that judge response by the number of hits on a Web site and not on the number of clickthroughs to specifics.

Hard-bitten old-timers point to the marketing fiasco of the Edsel automobile and New Coke as examples of the fallacy of market research. Actually, these point up the omnipresent gap between product and the attempt to sell that product. In both cases the advertising was superior. The target public rejected the product.

So the question "Just how do we learn what they want?" has to encompass not only exposure but what it is to which the target public is being exposed.

You may remember an agency/client story so well-known it has almost become folklore: British Rail executives visited an advertising agency that was vying for the account. The receptionist cracked her chewing gum, treated them like job applicants, and had them stewing in uncomfortable chairs. Just as they were about to leave in disgust, the agency principal appeared and explained that this treatment was deliberate: "We want to show you how *you* treat your customers." The revelation—as effective a piece of personalized "research" as could ever be brought into play—won the agency the account.

The moral of the story: Before researching advertising themes, research what is being sold and what the target consumer thinks of what is being sold. No amount of brilliant advertising can cause a potential customer or client to sample a product more than once.

The Obvious First Test

The key area in which testing and research overlap is the first test the marketer should apply to any product, any service, any cause: Will *anybody* want it?

In a twenty-first-century ambience that demands gigantic budgets for national product introduction and major budgets even for regional introduction, the astute marketer constantly looks for ways to eliminate the natural effervescence that attends internal staff reaction and replace that unbacked enthusiasm with the hard nut of fact. Focus groups may or may not supply valid information because of the artificial circumstance in which they are structured. As many marketers have learned to their eternal chagrin, research based on a "would you . . . ?" concept is as often invalid as it is valid.

Paid focus group attendees have the disconcerting habit of wanting to give the sponsoring company its money's worth. As is true of some juries, the bandwagon effect can sweep away results that might be illuminating, if negative. Responders to telephone questions are suspect immediately, not only because one cannot judge the ambience from which the answer comes forth, but also because the answer may be totally unbacked by prior knowledge or actual desire for use.

One-to-one, in-person questioning, too, has obvious holes in it. A shopper is accosted in the supermarket by a researcher with a clipboard: "Can you tell me why you chose that brand?" How likely to be valid is the answer if the reason was one of economics rather than actual desire? (The well-trained researcher knows the usual reason for choosing a generic against a name brand, regardless of the stated reason.) A traveler is accosted at the airport and asked opinions about a recently completed flight. Again the answers are suspect because they can be based on a single experience totally outside the orbit of airline capability or comfort. The late, legendary researcher Ernest Dichter made a telling comment about motivation research: "It can tell you a great deal . . . about the person asking the questions."

One other problem should be mentioned: The nature of interviewing cannot control the percentage of those who simply will not take the time to respond—and these may be the best prospects!

What, then, constitutes a logical first test of whether the product should go into the marketplace at all?

Major packaged-goods producers usually settle for a one-, two-, or three-market introduction, testing not only product but promotional techniques. Imperfect? It certainly is. Better than allowing internal enthusiasm to dictate a national launch? It certainly is.

A controverting opinion can come from those whose product has a time factor that can be damaged by delay. If the product is an improvement or upgrade over an existing product, the danger is obviously lessened, because the market has already accepted the concept.

Anyone who has shopped at Sam's Club or Costco has been confronted by table after table of edibles being introduced to the marketplace. A shopper picks up a free sample, tastes it, and nods approvingly. Is this a logical basis for determining market viability?

Obviously not. What matters is whether that shopper, half an aisle away, wheels her cart around to pick a can or box off the table adjacent to the sampling area.

The introduction of Universal Product Codes (UPCs) has sped up the process of reactive analysis considerably. The marketer can track, hour by hour, buying patterns and compare them with prior sales of similar items, and with the existence of advertising and couponing.

As we have explained elsewhere in this text, couponing gives an artificial boost to sales. In some cases, artifice becomes reality, and products such as cereals, yogurt, processed meats, pet foods, snacks, and soft drinks have become as dependent on these as magazines are for sweepstakes subscription promotions.

That a product fails in its initial testing phase does not mean that the product itself is defective. It also may mean that an educational process, alerting desired targets, has not yet taken hold (an indication of the value of dynamic public relations in product introduction). It also may mean that the promotional materials themselves have not been geared properly. With the plethora of new products swarming into the marketplace, those who use care and discretion—without allowing care and discretion to result in a snail's pace—are less likely to fail.

Predicting Response

Problem: A company advertised a telephone rate plan, using only direct mail and statement stuffers in order to avoid overloading the inbound telemarketing department. Response was so much heavier than anticipated that the telemarketers could not handle the volume and lost many responses.

Problem: An automobile manufacturer believed that its current model would be a strong seller in the marketplace. The company reached that conclusion without analyzing what other automobile manufacturers were producing and how they were pricing. Dealer inventories grew so dangerously bloated that the manufacturer was forced into a rebate program to reduce inventory.

In both cases, sophisticated marketers had reached projections based on apparent logic. In both cases, these projections were at variance with actual response. Sometimes missed projections are unavoidable, as happened when a Christmas collectible sold far better in a June test than in an October rollout.

This should suggest to any marketer whose product falls into a competitive arena—and this is close to 100 percent of all products—that the projection be tempered by both the novelty/excitement factor and close attention to what the competitors are doing. The danger, obviously, is that too much attention to competitor marketing tactics can result in a reactive posture instead of a proactive posture, which inevitably will lead to a secondary position in the marketplace.

We have seen that marketers can meet sales goals through artificial means, such as reducing prices, couponing, adding dealers and intermediaries, and expanding an advertising schedule. Each of these, if used to reach a sales goal that was predicted without anticipating their need, will skew the reality of a budget. Thus, although the sales goals may be met, the bottom line shrinks.

Predicting is a tricky business, and companies have filed lawsuits claiming that defecting employees carried with them information that enabled competitors to destroy the company's sales predictions.

Yet no one should assume that every person out there is going to buy one of something. Ultimately, much of the buyer's decision-making process occurs outside the orbit of advertising influence. The automobile manufacturer, then, says to the dealer, "This is your quota." The advertising agency says to its branch, "This is your quota." The department store says to its fashion salesperson, "This is your quota." Advertising, whose classic objective is exposure and recognition, in the twenty-first century adopts a heavier mantle: moving persuasion to its ultimate point.

Thus, the uneasy marriage between research and advertising may be a shotgun wedding, but the child of that wedding—reaching sales projections—can make a hero out of the reluctant husband.

The Obvious Benefit of Testing

The world of direct marketing reveres testing and often decries research. The philosophy underlying this attitude is obvious enough:

Research gives historical data; testing tells which approach is most effective.

Like most simplistic arguments, this one has a hole in it. A direct-marketing campaign may begin by testing one to twenty elements— for example, price, motivator, letter length, envelope treatment, use of color, number and type of enclosures, or typography. All of these will result in variations of response. None of these will indicate whether the offer itself is as valid as it might be.

Might it not also be possible to test the offer? Of course, and offer testing is not a novelty. But the notion of testing implicitly reflects a comparison of two or more elements, not a dispassionate, analytical study of what is being offered.

Certainly, testing is a greater specific than research because the results are instantly readable. By testing the price of a book at $29.95, $39.95, and $49.95, mailing 50,000 pieces with each price, the marketer in short order will have hard evidence of which price brings (a) the most total business; (b) the most total profit; and (c) the most returns and back-end troubles. Two pieces of information are lacking: (d) whether a $19.95 or $59.95 price might have been more profitable than any of the others; and (e) whether the subject of the book is valid for the target group.

One might conclude that both research and testing lack completeness, one without the other. Good point.

When and How to Test

The obvious time to test is at the moment of product introduction. Less obvious, but perhaps even more potentially profitable, is after a product has achieved a minimal niche in the marketplace, one the marketer wants to expand.

In the mail, testing is disciplined and specific. In media, readership and audiences are more polyglot and less controlled. This suggests different types of testing and demands professional analytical skills.

Example: A marketer mails 100,000 pieces of mail, 10,000 each to 10 lists, selling gourmet coffee. Quickly, that marketer will know which lists pulled best. To those lists new tests are constructed, each one an attempt to maximize response.

That same marketer might have the gourmet coffee in supermarkets. Retail action is spurred by a combination of broadcast commercials and print couponing. The results are considerably muddier, not only because the marketer has tried two separate elements coincidentally, but also because shelf position has a powerful effect on visibility, which in turn has a powerful effect on sales.

Is Global Research Possible?

Unquestionably, major brands have global aims beyond any marketing plans that could be implemented during the twentieth century. Will the product with a successful sales history in the United States have an equivalent victory in Brazil? In Japan? In Germany? In Turkey? Each of these requires a research project on its own.

Marketers still remember the disastrous introduction of laundry-softening dryer sheets in some areas of Europe. Why didn't the sheets have an even chance of achieving acceptance? Because the "carrier"—a dryer—was itself a rare acquisition. Softener sheets can't work with clothes hung out to dry on an outside clothesline.

A company called Research International has pointed out the possibility of incompatible studies, country to country. For example, in focus groups, young Asians tend to defer to the opinions of their elders, and mixed-gender sessions inhibit the free interchange of ideas. Similarly, a group that includes various executive levels can yield imperfect results because the lower-level executives may tend to toady to their supervisors. Research International also points out that in its experience, Latin respondents overstate their enthusiasm and Asians show diffidence.

Research is at the mercy of local convention and mores. Even discovering who in the household is the logical interviewee can change the results. For example, in the very highest economic circumstances in Brazil or Argentina, household products are below the level of interest of the householder. The best interviewee may very well be the housekeeper.

The Cutting Edge of Research?

An article in *Advertising Age* had this as its first paragraph:

> *Marketing research is undergoing a fundamental change, shifting from measures based on assumptions to ones that are more quantifiable, including whether people are actually buying products.*

The reference is to a system called advanced analytics, a mathematical modeling system that ties brand sales to the effectiveness of advertising. As stated earlier in this chapter, the technology—analysis of retail scanner data—has existed for some years. What has been improving has been the accuracy of the analysis itself.

The immediate result seems to be a reach for greater understanding of the relationship among individual media, total advertising budget, and performance in the marketplace. It would seem that this procedure is best applied to packaged goods.

In a nonmedia atmosphere, testing seems to be holding its premier position, if only because of the lesser budget involved and the shorter amount of time necessary to read results.

No sane person would dare to predict what advances in research and testing will take place during the next quarter century. Some of the most ancient methods, such as leaving samples at the door, achieve product usage without benefit of either media or market research. But what underlay the notion of producing these products in the first place?

Research has become high-tech, and results are increasingly timely and valid. Yet the number of market failures suggests that in no way has the value of research reached its pinnacle.

∎ 8 ∎

Evaluation: Relating Results to the Message— and to the Objectives

Crash.

Results are in. The campaign didn't work. The advertising didn't bring customers into the store or the showroom or to the telephone or fax machine or on-line URL.

The space buys and time buys were proper. We did reach the people who represented the biggest core of potential buyers or clients. The ads were handsome and clear. They weren't experimental, they weren't totally art-oriented, and they didn't cost a ton to produce. The product was on hand, and it was as advertised.

Crash.

What happened?

Monday-morning quarterbacking is a regular, if unfortunate, component of the advertising world. Answers aren't always clear-cut. Witness Snapple, a tasty soft drink that could not achieve a profitable percentage of market share despite millions of dollars spent to gain recognition. Marketed by Quaker Oats Company, the beverage brand was sold to Triarc Beverage Group in 1997, for what was described as the "bargain basement price" of $300 million.

One might conclude the obvious: A marketer, however powerful, cannot force consumers—or, for that matter, business targets—to accept what they don't want. The next logical question is whether the marketer should establish the desire as part of the overall advertising effort. This goes back to the ancient three-phase concept—pioneering, competitive, and retentive advertising. To this we might add a "pre" phase—a prepioneering phase—especially for a product attempting to carve a new niche of acceptance for its generic purpose as well as for its specific competitive posture.

One hole in the apparent logic, then, is the gap between recognition and buying impulse. These two terms aren't always in sync.

In the case of Snapple, Triarc, the new owner, apparently recognized that stimulation of buying demand required a major change of thrust. In early 1998, Triarc decided to use controversial radio personalities—Howard Stern for Snapple and Rush Limbaugh for Diet Snapple. The advertising budget was an estimated $30 million, which included line extensions. In addition to the radio schedule, both television and print were on the schedule. The editor of *Beverage Digest* was quoted as saying in early 1998, "Triarc has reversed the precipitous volume declines from the Quaker Oats era and has stabilized the brand." Snapple volume was down 5 percent in 1997 with a 15.8 percent share of the ready-to-drink tea market.

Fighting for Market Share

The gap between recognition and buying impulse is a gap in logic, surprisingly more often recognized by consumer targets than by advertis-

Loyalties are fragile and competition is intense in the world of fast-food restaurants. To help attract and hold customers, as one special promotion—such as a sweepstakes, figurines tied to a popular motion picture, or scratch-off cards—ends, another quickly begins.

ers. Without a call to action, "brand" isolates itself from the marketplace. Everyone knows Ivory soap; not everyone buys Ivory soap. The cola wars prove repeatedly that the actual taste of a soft drink is only one facet of the buying impulse.

Exemplifying the tight interrelationship between brand exploitation and generation of a buying impulse was the campaign initiated by Levi Strauss & Company to push its Dockers casual clothing to a level matching the sale of its jeans. Budgeted at $50 million, the campaign aimed itself at males aged twenty-five to thirty-four, a younger demographic than the typical Levi's promotion. The intention was not only to exploit within the specified demographic group, but also to take advantage of the anticipated market growth within Generation X and Echo Boomers.

To expand within other areas, Levi's increased the price of its jeans and mounted a campaign for its Silver-Tab line to compete with designer labels. Thus, marketing was adapted to keep pace with sociological developments.

The Ultimate Purpose of Advertising

Old-timers had a safe (and then valid) point: The purpose of advertising is not to sell but to place a product in a position in which those charged with the responsibility of selling can perform efficiently. In the twenty-first century, advertising agencies are either true marketing partners or the ex-agency of a client. The egg has been so thoroughly scrambled that many agencies now call themselves communications companies or marketing companies. Regardless of the appellation, the competitive nature of today's advertising climate demands marketing expertise beyond the ability to create and place advertising.

Establishing market share and increasing market share, then, are the twenty-first-century touchstones by which a company gauges the effectiveness of its advertising and promotion. Does this mean the venerable "noted" and "recall" yardsticks are obsolete? To some critics, the terms have been obsolete ever since the marketplace first realized that some of the best-remembered advertising messages were unable to increase the sales of whatever it was they represented.

Keeping score is necessarily half science and half "guess," not only because the public does not run on tracks, but also because the challenge often is to market a product or a service whose competitive position is weak or whose physical appeal is below the level of its competitors. Obviously, advertising is not parallel to manufacturing or distribution, nor should it be intended to overcome shortcomings in those two areas.

So the question "How do we increase market share?" requires an answer from every department, whether administrative, creative, production, media, database management, public relations, or research. (The very existence of a multiplicity of departments would confound the successful agency of half a century ago.)

The ever-looming "Why did it happen?" (or "Why didn't it happen?") has driven many agencies onto the open battlefield, where advertising executives masquerade as either point-of-sale merchants or customers. Thus, as we pointed out earlier, the old Campbell-Ewald agency was anticipating the twenty-first century when it required executives working on the Chevrolet account to visit a Chevrolet showroom for two weeks of the year to experience battle conditions.

Campbell-Ewald may have been prescient. An agency cannot today be a mere spectator to postadvertising activity, even if that activity is remarkably successful. The benefit of the intensified relationship is that an agency makes itself harder to replace. A client may easily switch creative sources, as clients have easily switched media-buying services, but replacing a marketing partner is major surgery.

"How Can We Prevent It?"

The danger of regarding disaster prevention as a major component of marketing is that the marketing team becomes so cautious it waits for the results from others before initiating an aggressive campaign on behalf of itself. In fact, the word *aggressive* may be itself too aggressive when describing an overly cautious marketing attitude.

The question "How can we prevent it?" in no way parallels "How can we repeat it?" Repetition, in the hands of a fast-acting marketing team, can solidify gains. Prevention can result in a disastrously shrunken market share.

Defensive marketing is reactive marketing, and history is on the side of those who act rather than react. Awareness of competition and what competitors might say or do or introduce or withdraw or adapt or cheapen or mutate differs from waiting for one of those possibilities to occur before implementing one's own programs.

Competing in a Mature, Saturated Marketplace

Product introduction often is the result of market saturation. Toothpastes first fluoridated, then whitened, then added peroxide, as inno-

This headache relief compound added a new dimension to sales by introducing a second packaging without changing its formula. Excedrin Migraine openly admits its formulation is identical to the traditional version but commands additional shelf space and new users.

vations no longer were innovative and demanded replacement in order to justify market expansion.

Credit cards added gold and then platinum in attempts to prevent slowdown due to market saturation. *The Wall Street Journal* commented that the consumer response to the 1997 blizzard of 3.01 billion credit-card mailings fell to a record low rate of 1.3 percent, down from what had previously been regarded as a very low response rate, 1.4 percent in 1996. The fourth quarter, in fact, fell to 1.1 percent. Did this indicate a falling off of credit card use? Not at all. Rather, it indicated a saturated marketplace in which a high percentage of new cards were issued to individuals who use them in place of existing cards—marching in place.

A market research company called Behavioral Analysis Inc. offered the opinion that the flood of platinum card offers put issuers "in the process of ruining a potentially new business. It took gold cards fifteen years to deteriorate. Platinum is doing it in a year." As readers of this book undoubtedly will observe, platinum cards in saturation are not the end of the issuance stream. New offers, using new hooks (diamond?), undoubtedly and necessarily will surface as credit card issuers continue the struggle for market share.

On an equally large scale, General Motors's share of the automobile market, once dominant, slid to a record low 31.3 percent in 1997, then fell even lower during the early months of 1998. Even though automobiles and trucks obviously are a mature marketplace, new-model introductions, in total, had not diminished. Those outside the GM orbit attributed the company's market erosion to two implicit problems:

1. Too many cars whose engineering and appearance seemed parallel with one another
2. Too long a lead-time to bring a new model into the marketplace

Recognizing the validity of these charges, General Motors executives reported that the switch to individual brand management, in which the managers are hand in glove with their designers and engineers, seems to have stemmed the slide. The system differs from prior Gen-

Freestanding inserts are popular media for timed promotions intended to increase product use through couponing. This one offers an option: a discount for buying two of the featured snacks, or free Coca-Cola for buying three. Sunday newspaper readers who might otherwise never consider a particular product carry the coupon to the supermarket for redemption.

eral Motors marketing/manufacturing methods in that the brand managers have both the authority and the opportunity to match their product to what new-car buyers have indicated they want.

In each of these cases—and in any case in which potential buyers grow bored and weary—the product and the way that product is sold are, actually, of a single piece. Advertising in the twenty-first century cannot successfully isolate itself from whatever is being advertised.

A True Marketing Partnership

The maturation of the advertising industry becomes complete with the third phase: the marketing partnership. From its beginnings as a media-buying service to its intermediate posture as the creator of the materials for which media have been bought to its twenty-first-century incarnation as salesperson, the advertising agency and/or in-house department already has begun to lose the word *advertising* from its name.

The result of this sophistication is not only the benefit of becoming less disposable—as any partner becomes less disposable than an employee would be—but also the inevitable spin-off of fragments from the whole. For example, the emergence of media-buying services and creative boutiques is a natural part of this evolution. In fact, many agencies regard their media-buying services as outside suppliers and sell them to nonclients and even other agencies on that basis.

Conclusion: The three-martini lunch has given way to the three-volume book of marketing procedures.

▪ 9 ▪

Poised
at the Edge
of the Springboard

Rip Van Winkle has no future as an advertising practitioner.

The advertising agency that lays claim to the position of "marketing partner" with its clients has to install the creative and technical expertise—*machinery* isn't an inappropriate term—to implement the claim. Otherwise, the agency, like other dinosaurs before it, will disappear, remnants surviving only as fossils.

Is the Future Already Here?

As decades meld into centuries, the function not only of an advertising agency but of advertising itself either keeps pace with the demands imposed by society—or disappears.

The era of the generalist in advertising (as in medicine, which has many parallels) is in eclipse. In the opinion of most marketing professionals (and to the consternation of one-person shops), that is the way it should be. If advertising is to be a profession and not a way station for dilettantes, it requires specialists with specialized education and talents.

The danger is as apparent as the benefit: Specialists tend to overemphasize their specialty and deny or ignore the value of activities outside their own orbit. So the successful advertising agency does retain a generalist. That person is (or should be) the chief executive officer, holding the reins and not allowing any subordinate to permit a specialized function to dominate where it shouldn't.

As new media such as the World Wide Web and global television began to take their place alongside traditional media, a potential danger appeared, as it did in the early days of television: Technicians had greater sway than marketers, and the medium often became the message. This is no cause for alarm, because history has shown with great regularity that technicians are executors, not originators. Dependence on novelty rather than salesmanship is, after all, the difference between attention getting and marketing: Getting attention is a component of marketing, but marketing may not necessarily be included in attention getting.

Truly Integrated Campaigns

As early as the 1970s, some of the major agencies adopted the term *integrated advertising.* What was wrong with their early definitions was not only the use of the word *advertising* instead of *marketing,* but also substitution of lip service for actual internal integration. What the agency really meant was it was offering a multiplicity of services, but those services weren't necessarily tied together in a coherent campaign. Within the agency, territorial fears generated a "Get off my turf!" attitude. Departments that represented lower direct income were relegated to a ghetto position in marketing planning . . . with attention given to the more glamorous and more immediately profitable media, whether those were the most logical marketing steps or not.

Agencies should not have been stunned when many of their better, most astute clients formed their own media-buying and direct-marketing departments and began internal exploration of Web site positioning.

The alarm call has not gone unheeded. As agencies mature into true marketing partners, they now absorb and implement these areas of marketing, even if not all represent immediate high-profit revenue streams. "Get off my turf!" is no longer even a questionable internal clarion call; it is lost in rewritten history, as the advertising profession becomes what it is supposed to be—a profession, with the professional demand for statesmanlike performance on all levels, in all departments, for all clients.

Brainstorming or Barnstorming?

The agency BBDO is usually credited with originating the brainstorming concept back in the 1960s. Brainstorming—having a roomful of people fire ideas with the only caveat being "No ridicule!"—certainly has resulted in uncovering marketing ideas that otherwise would have been buried because they originated at too low an echelon within the agency.

In too many cases, though, brainstorming has turned into barnstorming. The agency bombards its client with a multiplicity of creative concepts whose purpose, overt or covert, is to convince the client that the agency has a multiplicity of creative concepts. The filtration process lags behind the desire to prove that somewhere in the mix is the winning idea. Thus, instead of presenting a single creative execution to a client, today's agency typically transfers back to its client the decision of what will sell best, even though the client hired the agency because it has the people who know how to sell.

Obviously, those who pay the advertising bill are the ultimate decision makers. But compare this with the field of medicine: Would a doctor offer a patient a choice of surgeries? Actually, a doctor whose concern outweighed his or her ego would expose all options to a patient, reserving the role of adviser rather than dictator.

The issue becomes germane when a campaign loses impetus. In 1998, Nike abandoned its "I can" advertising strategy, with the CEO quoted as explaining, "Our problem has not been too much marketing, but too much ineffective marketing." The agency responsible for the campaign—one of several employed by Nike—lost position with this decision. But Nike did not make the decision arbitrarily; the company's net income was down 27 percent.

Was the agency to blame? Or was this a decision to shoot the messenger? Certainly it is common practice when profits or sales decline to reassess the relationship with the agency, regardless of who originated or implemented the creative concept. A sophisticated advertiser usually will have as much input into campaign strategy and tactics as the agency. This, in fact, does represent a true partnership. Agency/client relationships that have endured through multiple campaigns, some of which were more successful than others, reflect the spirit of a true partnership in which the results of brainstorming come under attack only if all suggestions are vetoed on grounds of incompetence.

In an era in which agencies can spend a quarter of a million dollars or more preparing a speculative presentation, a tightrope exists, and it's easy to fall off. Whatever the proposed marketing strategy and execution might be, the appearance has to differ from what has existed before, or the agency is out of contention. Yet, if the difference is too profound, the presentation can be rejected on the grounds that it represents barnstorming, not brainstorming.

Twenty-First-Century Relationships

The key to ongoing relationships, it has become clear, is not who can produce an ad at the lowest cost. Unquestionably that notion has resulted in thousands of short-term relationships. But in the twenty-first century, in which the cost of changing agencies can be as significant to a client as the loss of that client can be to the agency, the search for long-term marketing partners is the preferred way of doing business.

The agency, to be a genuine marketing partner, no longer can simply grind out ads like so much hamburger. Instead, the execution of creative concepts has to tie itself to the client's bottom line and the client's long-term marketing strategy, rather than the agency's trophy case.

BMW ran this full-page ad in *The Wall Street Journal*, using an award from a magazine as a touchstone. Following it is an ad that the automaker's U.S. advertising agency ran in the same issue.

HEY BMW, WE READ
THE BIG NEWS ON PAGE A5.
CONGRATULATIONS.

{ *Clients.*
All they care about is
winning awards. }

Fallon McElligott

The advertising agency placed this "congratulatory" ad in the same issue of *The Wall Street Journal* as its BMW ad. The line "Clients. All they care about is winning awards" is dry humor, but some may object to what seems to be a criticism.

This means leavening creativity with marketing awareness. The day of the "anything goes" creative department may necessarily go into eclipse because untempered creativity will not be a powerful enough weapon to compete with those advertising agencies that can offer true marketing partnerships through their depth and attention in areas such as sane research, product positioning, and attention to the competitive ambience in which all advertising exists today.

The near scandal attached to some media departments, in which underlings placed advertising in their favorite media whether or not those media were relevant to the clients' target groups, certainly has seen its day. Light shines on media plans, both internally and externally, and computer-programmed analyses quickly expose such peccadilloes.

The true marketing partner lives in both the present and the future, responding quickly to outside forces that can damage the effectiveness of both a campaign and a product or service the campaign is designed to promote. An example is a series of ads for veal that mirrored an earlier campaign which transformed the image of pork. Veal had been judged, not as meat but as cruelty to calves, with an intensively negative campaign by animal rights activists. The advertising bypassed these objections, reestablishing veal as an upscale entrée: "Transform any table into the Best Seat in the house." By running the ads in upscale publications such as *Bon Apétit* and *Restaurant Business,* the National Cattlemen's Beef Association, with a budget of only $1.1 million a year, achieved a 20 percent increase in veal consumption. Fur retailers, similarly, by taking the high road, bypassed the activist backlash. Advertising thus becomes proactive rather than reactive in a mixed ambience.

Advertising research truly comes of age when it contributes to the *anticipation* of trends and developments, instead of the traditional technique of contributing to a *reaction* to trends and developments.

Plight of the Small Competitor

Can a small agency compete as a full marketing partner?

Why not? The mergers and acquisitions that have spawned the behemoth agency empires have produced an interesting by-product: the specialized boutique.

Specialized boutiques now exist in every facet of the advertising/marketing mix. Creative boutiques, media-buying boutiques, research boutiques, design boutiques—all command a share of the market. Some clients (unimpressed by the marketing partner doctrine) prefer to pick and choose the outside services they require. They regard giant agencies as cumbersome, slow-moving, and expensive.

The New Age of Hypercompetitivism

Even as one corporate giant swallows another, assurance of continuing market share is less certain than it was a generation ago. Fragmentation of media and growing consumer and trade skepticism have opened opportunities for competitors whose knowledge of sales psychology can well outproduce the classic dependence on bulk.

One example is a 1998 campaign for Papa John's Pizza, which used a hard-hitting comparative television campaign to attack directly a considerably larger competitor, Pizza Hut. The difference, the campaign claimed, was that Papa John's used fresh tomatoes and Pizza Hut used tomato paste. Papa John's claimed that its pizzas won "significantly" in taste tests.

The effectiveness of the campaign was strong enough to wound the pizza franchise under attack and warrant their public objection. Pizza Hut said that Papa John's had skewed the tests by not including pan pizza, which Pizza Hut makes and Papa John's doesn't. The national advertising division of the Council of Better Business Bureaus, as arbiter, asked Papa John's to note that the tests did not include pan pizza but did agree that Papa John's had a "reasonable basis for its claim."

A more heavily publicized episode involved the number one fast-food franchiser, McDonald's. Departures from the venerable but workmanlike key line "You deserve a break today" have not been universally successful. In 1997, a campaign built around a fifty-five-cent promotion apparently was so unsuccessful that *Advertising Age* said the result damaged the agency's long-standing creative reputation. In fact, it may have contributed to the agency losing its position as lead agency.

Subsequently, a *Wall Street Journal* 1998 article pointed out that while McDonald's advertising budget increased 9 percent in 1997 (to $548.7 million), sales increased only 5.7 percent. The previous year, the advertising budget increased 17 percent and sales increased only 6.3 percent.

The new campaign at work during the period following the ill-fated fifty-five-cent promotion was "Did somebody say McDonald's?" Average sales at restaurants open at least thirteen months slipped for a third straight year. The question such a circumstance raises is, To what extent was the advertising at fault for the drop (or, had sales increased, for the rise)? What many critics quickly ignore is another factor, apparent in the Papa John's–versus–Pizza Hut promotion but not so clear in the McDonald's circumstance: what the competition is doing.

One competitor, Burger King, had been intensifying its marketing effort among juveniles through direct-mail birthday offers. Other fast foods, too, stepped up their marketing tempo, which suggests that an increase in budget may be necessary to maintain market share, let alone increase it.

The classic posture that the purpose of advertising is to generate exposure, not to be responsible for repeated sales of merchandise or fast food, may well have swung back into a valid position. That the public rejected McDonald's fifty-five-cent promotion may well have been due to muzziness and lack of clarity. That "Did somebody say McDonald's?" did not increase sales in ratio to the increase in budget is less attributable to the advertising itself than to lack of specials, premiums, and excitement that stimulate impulse visits as well as maintaining habitual visits.

McDonald's senior vice president of marketing, interviewed at the company's 1998 convention, said the chain would increase spending in radio, outdoor, and Internet, with all advertising mentioning the Web site. To shore up its most loyal diner group—children aged two to nine—McDonald's resurrected its once-ubiquitous clown, Ronald McDonald, pairing him with a Muppet-like partner, Iam Hungry. The

Beef up your incentive program.

Burger Bucks™ from Burger King®. The reward that your employees can enjoy anytime, anywhere.

CALL: 1-800-535-3412

©1997 Burger King Corporation.

Advertising Burger Bucks as employee incentives represents a marketer's effort not only to establish another profit center but also to increase store traffic, with the possibility of planting the seed of repeat visits.

two "starred" in a video made available for $2.99 with the purchase of a McDonald's Happy Meal. As a way of expanding its dollar volume, the company announced line extensions—for example, a branded ice cream and bottled water. Curiously, franchisees seemed to endorse the "Did somebody say McDonald's?" approach, isolating it from the gap between budget and volume.

A new character, Iam Hungry, joined venerable Ronald McDonald in McDonald's determined effort to continue its supremacy as the fast-food restaurant of choice among young children. An entertaining video accompanied the introduction of this character.

Competition: The Ultimate Determinant

As the "burger battles" and "pizza peccadilloes" seem to show, advertising often is the scapegoat for lagging market share. Such advertising giants as Nike seem to have shown unease when sales do not maintain a level they regard as satisfactory. But in many of these cases, aggressive competition not only overrides a market leader's budget but forces reevaluation on all levels. One wry commentator compares blaming an agency when a company's brand loses impetus to firing the manager when a baseball team is in a hitting slump.

Burger King, quickly recognizing a marketing opportunity, reacted to the apparent faltering of McDonald's by junking its "Get Your Burger's Worth" slogan, which it had used for some three years, in favor of "It Just Tastes Better." As McDonald's announced a shift back to local advertising, Burger King announced an increase in national advertising.

Is, after all, the success of any brand based on its ability to outadvertise its competitors? The jury certainly is still out. A major indicator will be the ultimate result of competitive advertising in the area of electric power. The traditional giant suppliers are being forced at press time to compete for the first time with independents whose entire approach to marketing is that they can supply identical electrical power to consumer, business, and industrial customers for a lower price.

If exposure to such a message—getting the identical item for less—were the sole motivator, mass defections surely would occur. Ample history has shown such a conclusion is specious. Over the years since AT&T lost its exclusive telephone franchise, others have eroded the company's market share but haven't driven it to the point of being a secondary supplier, even though almost all its rivals offer a direct price comparison.

In the case of electric power, whether established brands can be unseated solely by a price comparison is certainly questionable. Sophisticated marketers—including many of AT&T's competitors—can testify that price is only one facet of the marketing mix affecting a switch of loyalty, however fragile that loyalty may be.

Whether the product is fast food, electric power, automobiles, or designer jeans, the competitive nature of the marketplace boosts image to a point of equivalence with price. The most eye-catching and attention-getting campaigns can wear thin, and the curious relationship between advertising budget, advertising cleverness, ability to build rapport with advertising targets, and what is actually being sold represents a scrambled egg that defies analytical descrambling.

As Papa John's and Pizza Hut engaged in their intramural argument, a different kind of attention was awarded to Taco Bell, a fast-food franchise specializing in Mexican takeout. This campaign emphasized a speaking Chihuahua dog rather than any menu item. The result was a satisfying flow of diners into Taco Bell. That a simultaneous demand arose for Chihuahua T-shirts indicated that response was to the campaign, not necessarily to the menu.

A parallel is the M&Ms phenomenon. Introduction of new colors and assignment of "personality" to each color was measurable in store sales of the individual colors. Again, campaign superseded product in establishing a buying attitude. And, again, an entire catalog of ancillary merchandise achieved a popularity that never could have been possible had the advertising centered itself on such traditional factors as taste and nonmeltability.

Multiple Competitions: The Challenge of the Twenty-First Century

Advertising and marketing have traveled light-years beyond the days of a handful of basic media. Just as radio added an entire new spectrum of media decision-making options, and as television complicated these options as no medium had ever done before, and as cable and satellite further complicated the broadcast option universe, and as online advertising confounded many whose training and background were threatened, so does a bewildering array of media possibilities confront the twenty-first-century advertiser. Add to this an equally bewildering array of competitors in almost every field of choice—for example, financial services and credit cards, fast foods, transportation, packaged goods, and discount stores—and one sees how the burgeoning marketing partnerships between the advertising agencies and their clients are more delicate than marketing logic should dictate.

Unquestionably, an advertising campaign that fails to seize and excite interest is a red flag in the relationship, because the traditional posture of an advertising agency is itself exposed as less than effective.

Unquestionably, too, as a marketing partner, the advertising agency (or "marketing agency") cannot bear sole responsibility for a product or service that either ages or loses glamour. For generations consumer and business targets have proved the impossibility of advertising a client's wares into a position of dominance when those wares themselves are worthy only of a sampling and not of an ongoing buying pattern.

Does this mean that as the twenty-first century ripens, advertising and marketing counselors must broaden both their talents and their influence to extend to what they are selling as well as the means by which they sell it? Does it mean that media, in turn, have to present hard justification not only for their existence, but for their usefulness on a case-by-case basis?

If your personal conclusion is "probably," you may well be in the vanguard of a new wave of marketing expertise. Advertising, like medicine, not only has reached a plateau of sophistication in which specialists are necessary; it also has reached a point of logic in which the various components of its own structure had better integrate and complement one another on a statesmanlike level. Competitors unable or unwilling to reach this level may well have a difficult time of it.

Interesting times ahead, don't you think?

Interview with Charles D. Peebler Jr.

President, True North Communications Inc.
New York

Mr. Peebler, we are seeing an extraordinary sequence of events: Agencies are swallowing agencies, and the consolidation of power, buying power, and creative power is in the hands of very few. Do you regard this as ultimately—please note that word ultimately—*favorable for the advertising profession?*

Porsche is arguably the finest automobile manufacturer in the world today. (Strike the word arguably.) But the company is soon to be **without an advertising agency** to create awareness and excitement for the brand. And so, in the time-honored tradition of a shark feeding frenzy, every agency worth its pants is furiously trying to figure out the new business kit, the **keen insight** into the Porsche brand, the nugget of marketing brilliance that might curry enough favor to land a spot on Porsche's shortlist. But Porsche has just relocated from Reno to Atlanta, and in the midst of unpacking flatware and taking a good hard look at the Atlanta public school system, they have **understandably delayed their review.** When you factor in the realities of a new business pitch, Porsche may very well

Why we should all buy a Porsche.

be without any new brand advertising for quite some time. Some people think Porsche doesn't need advertising. **"Hey, those babies practically sell themselves."** And while they make a good point, those laypeople and daydreamers are forgetting the basic tenet of our proud but beleaguered industry: **Without advertising, even the best brands will eventually die.** And if that happened to Porsche it would be a tragedy. And there would be no review. So, how can we help? How can we see Porsche through its time of vulnerability? Well, if this advertising community is indeed a "community," we'll stop with our self-absorbed new-business shenanigans, and we'll do something Porsche really will appreciate. **We'll all buy Porsches.** It's so simple. We won't craft expensive 150-pound brushed-aluminum credentials packages designed to dazzle Porsche with tales of our agency's strategic brilliance in the face of many complex marketing challenges in both the national and the global arenas. We'll buy **Boxsters.** We won't send our entire planning department to Stuttgart with Hi8 video cameras. We'll **cancel that boondoggle** and get on a waiting list for the '99 **Carrera.** We won't spend $60,000 on a five-minute rip-o-matic of stock footage and cross dissolves that concludes with a tasty title card with our agency's name and phone number followed by a scene from the quintessential 80s coming-of-age movie where the lead character said, "Porsche, there is no substitute." We'll spend $72,000

on a new Porsche 911 Carrera Targa! If you believe the Red Book (and we sure do), there are about 5,000 advertising agencies in this great country. And if each agency set a goal of purchasing only two Porsches, together, over the next 12 months, we could **raise Porsche sales by roughly 77%.** Seventy-seven percent sales growth, during a period with no new image advertising? Fantastic. And the best part of this plan? **We'll all own Porsches.** The finest motor cars on the road today. Take the '98 911 Carrera 4 AWD Cabriolet, for example. According to a brochure we read, it dramatically combines the enjoyment of open-air motoring with the traction and road-holding of Porsche's all-wheel-drive system. What senior creative director doesn't enjoy open-air motoring? Or the '98 Boxster. It boasts a 201 horsepower 2.5-liter engine, four-wheel independent suspension and four-wheel disc brakes with an anti-lock braking system. The **average middleweight hotshot copy writer flush with award-show success and bonus money could ease behind the wheel of one of these babies for about $42,000** (slightly higher fully loaded). And we can look beyond our agency walls. We can call our rich clients. Our rich production company friends. The highly paid celebrity talent and voice-over kings we've turned into landed gentry. We

The finest motor car on the road today.

can tell them all what a fantastic car Porsche is. **Get them excited about the Porsche brand.** After all, isn't that our job? Together, we can have a real impact on the Porsche business. We can help them sell cars in the most direct way possible. **By buying cars.** And if, at the end of the day, Porsche invites any of us to pitch their fine account in appreciation for what we've done for them, well sir, that's just gravy.

Paid for by Wieden & Kennedy New York

This ad appeared in *Advertising Age* at a time when Porsche was interviewing agencies. The intention, obviously, was to gain attention and inclusion in the review, but the automobile manufacturer selected another agency.

CHARLES PEEBLER: That's hard to look at, because you have to put *favorable* in context. I think it's favorable because it will provide survival of the fittest, because our industry has had to consolidate, like the clients that we serve. And if you look at the industry, client consolidation is going on right and left. For example, we have the merger of Chrysler and Mercedes.

You just go down the line, and they expect agencies to be more efficient, more effective, more global in serving them. We looked at some statistics the other day. There are now twenty-three clients spending over a billion dollars a year on advertising, and those are multinational clients seeking multinational representation.

This whole trend as we see it will end up most likely with four or five—some say maybe six—mega-agency holding companies, and they will be in control, really, of the multinational clients throughout the world.

Also, we see a consolidation in terms of media buying. Some people say media buying will distill itself to a point at which four or five media-buying groups will buy most of the media. But there will also always be room for small, specialized, local agencies, in my opinion, to work with start-up companies and things of that nature.

Is it favorable? It's favorable because it is in essence what we have to do to preserve the agency's role in industry. So, yes, overall I would say it's favorable.

You adopted the phrase media neutral *as a description of optimal agency service to a client. Can you explain the term* media neutral *and how it differs from previous agency services?*

C.P.: *Media neutral* may not be a good term because it's an internal term, and what it says is, We believe that there is an obligation on the part of our people in servicing client needs to take an unbiased approach to the client's budget and to look at the breadth of things that we can do for a client, to communicate. What we have gone to in terms of some wording now is to say that it's *bonding,* not branding. That counts because it encompasses media neutrality. What we are saying is, "Let's look at a consumer and let's look at our client or our client's products and services, and let's determine how we can bond those two things together," the process of bonding being a proactive way of one-on-one putting a product or service together with the consumer.

Bonding involves a broad list of potentials that involves more than media advertising. It's more than public relations. It's more than direct [marketing]. It's more than promotion. It's more than establishing brand identity and giving personality to it. It's putting all those things into a package that surrounds and bonds that customer to your product.

Is it then true that the term advertising agency *may be a dinosaur?*
C.P.: Well, yes and no. We kind of stay within the holding company concept. We have a series of services that provides solutions.

I don't want to go to somebody and sell integration. I want to sell problem solutions. And we believe it's incumbent upon us, looking at clients today, to try to determine how we can best assist them in getting a return on their investment. That means optimizing their expenditures in those things that will best bond that customer to their product. So media neutrality was born from the concept that says, "Let's look at that same approach," saying, "Let's go with no biases, let's start on a zero basis at all times and determine what factors allow us to bond a customer to our product."

In marketing and advertising, as in medicine, for example, the general practitioner seems to be disappearing in favor of a bunch of specialists. With the growth of specialized talent and resources, in your opinion how can the twenty-first-century agency prevent intramural jealousy—battles for supremacy—in presenting marketing concepts to a client?
C.P.: The key to providing media neutrality is to have a generalist who can take a broad view—understand the consumer, understand the consumer's needs, and provide ways and solutions to best reach them and bond with them. The specialist most likely is not going to do that, but once you get down to how best to approach that customer, you then want to call upon the specialist to apply his specialty in conjunction with everything else, so there is a unified image bonding that customer to the product.

So the generalist who controls this is a "supreme account executive"?
C.P.: I guess you would call that person an account executive. I don't know a better term yet, but it would be some term that includes being a manager of brand bonding.

How does one become a manager of brand bonding? What kind of background would make sense?

C.P.: Well, I think the background has to be one of breadth. They have to be strategic in nature. Obviously, they have to have an understanding of clients. They may have come out of planning, which may be a very good source for that type of person in the future because they have to have a broad outlook. They have to have a strategic outlook. But most of all, they have to have a good grounding in the consumer that you are trying to reach and an understanding of that consumer. Because if we don't focus on the end need, which is really how our product or service gets into the consumer's life, we will miss the boat by a large margin.

Some marketers, some clients, are going to be handling through their own internal departments some of those specialized areas of marketing like direct or the Internet or point-of-purchase. What is the agency reaction to that procedure?

C.P.: Well, I believe clients should do anything they can do, if they can truly do it effectively and efficiently.

I think agencies do have an opportunity. We've seen many cases where people take something in-house to see it become less energized, more departmentalized, and narrowcast in terms of the way it's looked at with substantially less creativity involved in the process. If you can overcome all those things, then certainly, from a logic standpoint, there are things that can be done internally; we don't have to go externally. The problem is like so many things: The concept sounds right and potentially is right, but in more cases than not, it lacks reality when you get to execution because of the inbred nature of internal departments. They get off in a very narrow focus, and as I say, in most cases the internal execution lacks the creativity that our business seems to generate when you live in an external world. And you have to maintain the discipline of knowing it isn't what you did yesterday but what you are going to do tomorrow that makes a difference.

The concept of cost per thousand has been under attack by critics who say it's obsolete and nonrepresentative. Your comment?

C.P.: I think when you are dealing with cost per thousand, you generally are talking about awareness or potential awareness. And if we go to bonding, we've gone so much further then that we should be talking about targeted customers. We should be talking about sales. We should be going more to one-on-one and how do we get to them. And so I think we are entering an age where we still have to look at some cost per thousands, but I think they are becoming less meaningful as we become more targeted, more focused, and use more direct methods of selecting ways of talking to customers on a one-to-one basis.

I don't know what the measurement is, but there should be a measurement that says, "You know, it's not how many I get exposed to but the fact that in this particular medium I can talk to 30 percent of the people I know who are really potential heavy users of my product, with whom I have to find the ways to bond." I would rather have "bonders per thousand" or something.

The 15 percent agency commission is gradually disappearing. How do you envision agency compensation evolving as advertising agencies become marketing agencies?
C.P.: I think there are two factors: Obviously, we really don't look at 15 percent anymore. We look at compensation from the standpoint of running a business: What is our gross income, and how can we manage that gross income to generate the right result for a client? So wherever that revenue comes from, it's "What is the revenue, and therefore what can you afford to spend on staffing to provide service?" Obviously when that's done, the agency has to be able to make a profit so that it can invest in people and do the things it needs to do to maintain a competitiveness and to maintain objectivity and to maintain the knowledge basis upon which creativity is dependent.

In order to do that, I don't think you can just go to a straight hourly basis either. So I believe that clients have to provide incentives, even if we go to more of a fee system.

So the agency becomes a true marketing partner?
C.P.: That's what I believe. People have said to me, "What do you do? Do you measure sales?" Sales may be one link. But is it a good measure when you know that if somebody raises or lowers the price, they impact sales greatly?

I prefer to say to the clients we work with, "I want to have the same system of reward for the agency that you have as a member of client management." They have the same goals, the same objective; we get evaluated on the same basis. And if my client gets 20 percent of his annual compensation as his bonus, I think the agency should have the potential for a 20 percent bonus if they contribute what they have contributed, working with the client to achieve the goals that will get his bonus or her bonus.

Does that mean that each client is approached on an individual level, with no template?
C.P.: I think it has to mean that, because if we look at what we can do for a client in a world of bonding, where we start without bias and have media neutrality, what we are really saying is that we don't know what is going to get you greatest return on investment in terms of how we approach it. And that should be our focus—to be as efficient and effective as we can be.

What we are talking about is solving problems and providing solutions that help you reach your goals and objectives as a client. If you reach those, then there should be a success fee, and that will allow us then to invest in the things that will allow us to keep that process moving forward on a positive basis, to develop strengths and capabilities for the clients we serve.

Let's talk global. The twenty-first century certainly will bring forth global marketing as a major factor. How profound an effect will the introduction of a single currency in Europe, the Euro, have on the concept of global marketing?
C.P.: The way we look at the world today is that there are about fourteen markets in the world where roughly 75 percent to 80 percent of all the marketing spending takes place. And we tend to look and break down the world by regions, and there are, say, four or five countries in Europe, three countries in Asia, three in Latin America, and so forth. And, of course, the United States is a major force. When you look at that, you say that's more or less the universe that makes up truly 80 percent of marketing going on in the world. So if four or five of those countries are in Europe, a single currency should help and have a profound effect on some of the marketing and how it transpires.

The other side of that is I'm not so sure, and it will be interesting to see what happens. As you have a single currency, you will have ease on the one hand, but I'm not so certain at least in the short term that it won't as a result cause a rising nationalism. The price in the currency may be the same, but the need to individualize to countries may increase because there's an attitude: "How do we maintain the character in our roots in a changing world?" This sometimes becomes more important.

A few years back, there were maybe 100 countries in the world. Today there are close to 200 countries. Some say in another ten or fifteen years we could have 300 countries as we experience some splintering. One of the other things that's going on in the world today is a reverse migration of people who have been in pockets. Germans in Albania, for example, are returning to Germany as people become more nationalistic. It's a strange thing to watch, but my guess is short term it's going to facilitate business in one sense while causing a rising nationalism in the other.

How does an agency equip itself to become global?
C.P.: I think it has to equip itself, first of all, with a mental attitude. It has to broaden itself. It has to truly become global.

If we're media neutral, we've got to become country neutral and say it doesn't make any difference where a sale comes from. It's which of those sales can be made in the most efficient, effective, and profitable manner for the client. And we have to have people who have traveled and are broad-based enough to understand and accommodate that approach to life.

And certainly when we have the Internet and other elements that are now becoming truly global media, the process is going to be facilitated. I think we're going to be amazed fifty years from today with what we see.

We also will evolve from a country where "diversified" is already important today, but by 2040 or so the character of the United States will be entirely different because what we call minority today will be the majority. And I think as a result we will have a much greater understanding and appreciation for diversity, and that will certainly be a different challenge for us as we move forward.

You said earlier that there will always be a niche for the small agency. How does a small agency survive in an era of computerized bulk media buying and specialized talents global coverage?
C.P.: There could be alliances. A local agency in the United States could be a $600 million agency, but it is going to be a local agency. And to do

certain things, they may have to have alliances or partnerships in order to provide their clients with the most efficient and effective way of doing business. If there are three or four media-buying groups in the world, those smaller agencies are going to have to somehow have an alliance or a partnership with one of them in order to secure the right rates for clients.

I would say also what the agency has to do is to have a clear-cut understanding of who they are and what they do and focus on those things, because obviously they can't lose their focus and try and be something that they aren't. If they do that, they'll lose very rapidly. So survival will require a much better understanding of what you are and how you are set up and what you can in turn claim to clients and prospects that you do better than anyone else.

The last question—and you have hinted at some of the answer: Look ahead halfway into the twenty-first century and speculate on the composition of the typical advertising agency in the year 2050.
C.P.: I think in 2050 the agency will still be the core of creativity, and it will be manned by people who are extraordinary in their questioning, in their ability to look at things in juxtaposition. It will be an agency where you will see people working at computers. It will not look like an agency today; the agency will have to work at how they get people to team, because they will be sitting there in front of computer screens flashing messages to each other in an instantaneous method and will be doing it on a global basis.

You will be sitting there writing copy with an art director in Thailand, and it will all be going on simultaneously. It will be an exciting time. It will have us doing more things on a broader basis of media than we've ever done. We will have abilities to get into this bonding in a way never thought possible in terms of individualizing messages—responding and interacting with those consumers for clients.

We may be writing messages for individuals of a certain type and changing them as the day goes on, based on what that consumer does that day. And potentially the channels of distribution will be entirely different.

We can see a day when so many things would be individualized that some of the freestanding major high-cost retail outlets that are main-

tained today would no longer exist. You might well be able to get anything from an automobile to apparel. I can in virtual reality put on various clothes, try them on. Through the computer, I can order them, and
they can be cut to my order and shipped to me in a matter of days or
even hours, all personalized. The future is going to cut out whole
avenues of distribution.

In the same token there will be a higher need for agencies with specialized talents to customize those messages with an understanding and
ability to manipulate data, make those data work, and then tailor messages that will draw favorable responses, because there won't be some
of the personal interaction that has existed in the past.

Now you'll say to me again, "Is that favorable or not?"

I don't know. But I think that is where we're headed.

End with
a Chuckle!

The authors thank Ray Schultz, Editor-in-Chief of the magazine *Direct,* for allowing them to reprint this gem, a flawless commentary on the profession we all love so much.

How many account executives does it take to change a lightbulb?
How many can we charge for?

How many database managers does it take to change a lightbulb?
First we compile profiles and decide on total units of response, then we can back out a number.

How many art directors does it take to change a lightbulb?
Does it have to be a lightbulb?

How many writers does it take to change a lightbulb?
Change? I'm not changing crap. Who wants to change it? Is it an authorized change?

How many creative directors does it take to change a lightbulb?
Bulb? I'dunno. I have to catch a plane to Chicago. You guys handle it.

How many photographers does it take to change a lightbulb?

First off, it's not a real lightbulb and it will cost $950 more if we change it.

How many print production buyers does it take to change a lightbulb?

Forget it. There's not enough in the budget to even think about changing it.

How many junior account administrators does it take to change a lightbulb?

I was told it was supposed to be changed last week. But I wasn't told until today. Someone goofed. It's not my fault. I didn't even realize that there was a lightbulb. Maybe you told whatzername and she forgot to tell me. But I'll change it *now* if it has to be changed. Is there a memo on it? Where's the ladder? Or do I use a chair? I could fall. But that's OK, I'll change it if I'm supposed to. Who changed it last time?

APPENDIX A

Marketing to African Americans

New Realities Today, New Visions for Tomorrow

by Stedman Graham, President and CEO, GGB

America is entering a period of profound change. To put it simply: in the lives of today's toddlers, the world's leading nation will change from a 25 percent minority population to a minority-majority. This kind of unprecedented, rapid shift will influence all institutions from politics to plays, from entertainment to education, from leadership to leisure.

—Eric Miller, *From Melting Pot to Magnet: The American Diversity*

The face of our country is evolving right before our eyes, and the smart advertisers and their agencies will recognize and act on that transformation. Some already acknowledge the statistics on ethnic population growth and annual buying power, and their marketing communications contain more images featuring people of color. Other firms have probably developed vague mid- to long-range plans on how to deal with this highly visible phenomenon. But overall, there are not enough marketers who share the vision of the vast opportunities ahead.

This is the basis for the growth of agencies specializing in integrated marketing communications programs targeted to ethnic consumers, especially those with an emphasis on the Hispanic or African-American marketplace. Such specialists have a singular definition of *vision*—the ability to see what is invisible to others. But what could be invisible about the African-American marketplace, representing 34 million people and the single largest minority group in the United States? What is it that some of the world's most respected marketers don't yet perceive?

They must recognize the enormous changes going on around them. This new world that they have assumed was five or ten years down the road is already at their doorstep. The story of the "new America" isn't just a prediction; it's happening right now. Marketing to this new America means the end of business as usual, and what they should acknowledge is that the time to get on board—to build brand loyalty, to forge connections with this powerful, emerging segment of consumers—is now. Those slow to do so risk being left at the gate.

What we are seeing is a total paradigm shift. Truly savvy marketers realize that what worked for them in the past will not automatically win them new customers in the future. There's a whole new set of rules for selling to this new America—a two-way, relationship-oriented model of advanced integrated marketing that respects, reflects, and contributes to both cultural and community values. And while this rings true for a broad spectrum of ethnic constituencies, it is especially true for the African-American consumer marketplace.

The Story Beyond the Numbers

The sheer magnitude of the numbers alone testifies that the African-American marketplace offers significant opportunity. Here are some 1998 numbers: Representing over $460 billion in annual buying power (up 54 percent since 1990), the African-American market is the fastest-growing economic segment in the United States. Nearly 50 percent of African-American consumers can be considered middle class (up from 16 percent in 1990). There are currently over 34 million African-American consumers; this number is expected to grow at a rate of 44 percent over the next twenty-five years. In fact, African Americans alone will account for 30 percent of the total U.S. population growth through 2005.

Over the past decade, African Americans have demonstrated increased consumer spending power. Although the group as a whole has not achieved parity with nonethnic consumers in terms of disposable income or per-capita spending, African Americans have been responsible for a share of retail sales growth well exceeding their percentage of the population in several retail categories, including purchases of new cars, household appliances, apparel, personal products, and food away from home. Additionally, along with their buying power, these consumers have new saving power and are rapidly becoming an attractive new market for our newest client, the Securities Industry Association.

One case in point: The growth rate of African Americans purchasing new cars is twelve times that of nonblack purchasers over the last decade. The latest figures also show African-American per capita spending is virtually equal to nonblack spending in the major household appliance, furniture, and grocery categories.

This indicates a tremendously viable market segment, strong today and poised for enormous growth in the future. There's just one very important catch: Marketing to an African-American audience is significantly different from marketing to a general or mainstream audience. Marketers who ignore this crucial reality do so at their own risk. When this nation's current minorities eventually do become the majority, ignoring the rules of marketing to the new America will not be an option. So it's best to get started building your base right now.

No More Business as Usual

Unfortunately, several companies think that slipping African-American or other ethnic faces into what is otherwise a traditional ad campaign will do the trick. They are in for a rude awakening. Marketing messages targeted to African Americans require an elevated level of cultural awareness; otherwise the messages risk reinforcing ethnic stereotypes and alienating the very consumers they are intended to persuade.

Take a traditional execution for a personal deodorant showing a young man running late for work, or an ad for a household cleaner featuring a housewife battling a messy kitchen. Dropping in an African-American face could set off alarms about old racial stereotypes. GGB recently met with a company preparing a marketing effort directed toward young black males. We stressed the importance of building relationships with their audience. There were certainly various ways to do this without resorting to featuring a "homeboy" with a boom box on his shoulder in their ad executions.

These types of portrayals are *not* the way to induce African Americans to embrace a marketer's product or service. It is a matter of plain common sense to realize that cultural orientation has a profound influence on how certain messages are received.

African Americans are a very media-savvy group. We are not only heavy consumers of broadcast media (research indicates, for example, that we watch 73.5 hours of television a week versus the national average of 48.5 hours), but discerning consumers. Our media consumption habits have helped develop a heightened sense of whether or not the messages aimed at us are authentic. It's important for African Americans to see themselves in ads (70 percent of African Americans say they're more likely to respond to an advertisement or an endorsement from a black actor or celebrity), but an execution that displays ignorance of cultural nuances or motivators can easily backfire.

For instance, a broadcast execution or print ad that features a group of black women who are all "plus" sizes or are all light-skinned can inadvertently turn off a target audience that resists being generalized. Ads that overlook the diversity of shades and sizes within the African-American community can trigger responses such as, "You don't really understand African Americans; you haven't taken the time to get to know me."

This sense of awareness extends to media placement as well. Consider the top ten television programs watched by African Americans versus those watched by all others. There's only one show common to both groups. Building a solid relationship with African-American consumers requires a targeted media approach. Marketers must make commitments to broadcast and print media that offer a special relevance to the African-American community, rather than hoping to succeed just by throwing media weight at them or incorporating black consumers in broad-based media plans.

A Question of Respect

Faced with these issues, some marketers bristle. "African Americans are too sensitive," they say. "Why should my marketing plan for African Americans be so radically different? I don't need a separate plan for Italian Americans or Irish Americans. We're all Americans, aren't we?"

Absolutely. We are all Americans—and proud of it. But African Americans are keenly protective of their cultural heritage and can be more suspicious of assimilation than other ethnic counterparts. According to research conducted in 1996, nearly 70 percent of African Americans surveyed felt "the need to sustain ethnic traditions and symbols," as opposed to 46 percent of all other respondents; 78 percent believed "parents should pass on ethnic traditions," versus 62 percent of all others; and 90 percent of African Americans agreed with the statement "I am proud of my ethnic heritage," compared to 78 percent of all others.

The key issue, however, can be summed up in one word, an attribute cherished by African Americans: *respect*. Respecting the consumer is a given in all marketing outreach, but it is even more vital when building a relationship with the African-American market. African Americans have developed a finely tuned radar for media portrayals that lack an in-depth understanding of black culture, heritage, and institutions.

Another example: Separate yet related research has shown that over 60 percent of African Americans cite respect as the reason they choose one retailer over another. In focus groups relative to retail stores, GGB found African Americans swearing off certain department store chains forever, not due to merchandise selection or pricing, but due to what they saw as patterns of disrespect: being followed by salesclerks, being steered away from certain brands, and being told, "That's too expensive."

Doing Well by Doing Good

One of the best ways marketers can demonstrate their respect for the values of African Americans is to support cause-related programs that help our communities, especially those that honor or celebrate our cultural heritage and pride of accomplishment. The business concept of "doing well by doing good" enjoys its greatest success when used with emerging markets. African Americans are highly responsive to organizations and efforts that give something back to the community, viewing the efforts as a gateway to mutual respect, rather than an attempt to exploit the market solely as a revenue opportunity.

It's not philanthropy, but a simple economic formula: Align with causes and events that strengthen the foundation of African-American communities. Do so in a manner that respects cultural heritage and values, and your company can gain the respect needed to forge the brand loyalty essential to long-term customer relationships. This is a win-win situation for all involved.

GGB put this theory into practice when we helped introduce the Diahann Carroll brand of apparel, the first celebrity signature clothing line launched by an African-American woman. Instead of renting out a lavish reception hall, we scheduled the line's gala debut at a newly opened department store in the Bronx, located in a revitalized neighborhood that had long awaited the return of a major retail outlet to serve their growing needs. Although the event was attended by several celebrities, we, as organizers, made certain to set aside time in the program to recognize members of the community—pastors, teachers, neighborhood leaders whose contributions made a significant difference in the lives of area residents. These actions helped elevate the event from just another glitzy party to a source of civic pride.

Similarly, the firm is now organizing such events as the Djoliba Festival, a global event saluting the African diaspora, featuring the work of black artists and entertainers from around the world, and the National Black Fine Arts Show, a prestigious showcase for the talents of African-American artists. GGB is incorporating numerous community-based initiatives in its African American–focused advertising and promotional programs for clients such as Taco Bell, JCPenney, and Bausch & Lomb.

Some Guiding Principles

Effectively targeting this segment in the coming years will in my opinion rely on the adoption of a few basic principles:

- Develop cohesive strategies in which advertising, marketing, sales, and promotions are geared toward the same strategic goal. Work to develop a synergy with the total promotional effort.
- Create a dynamic network of strategic alliances, and use the powerful new information systems to manage these virtual organizations and businesses.
- Empower and create other opportunities in interdependent relationships.
- Work as the hub that unifies partnerships to provide ongoing support, cutting-edge research, customized programming, and strategic marketing while linking clients to a vast network of expertise. Marketers can explore specific challenges and develop alternative solutions through broadened perspectives.
- Understand that globalization requires that all organizations will eventually have access to breakthrough technology. The future, therefore, will belong to those who can tap into the creative potential for their people. Networking, support systems, and grassroots marketing allow you to gain this access.

Time to Act

Ethnic agencies were created to help major marketers meet the challenges posed by this emerging "minority-majority." We can safely predict that, in the near future, more and more marketers will begin to seek out advertising and communications partnerships structured along this model: integrated marketing specialists who represent a bridge between grassroots communities and the *Fortune* 500—a partnership of organizations combining intimate knowledge of the ethnic marketplace with the established resources and reach of a major multinational communications powerhouse. Few if any such hybrids exist in the marketplace right now; however, more are sure to follow as the need for their services grows.

A Classic Agency Approach to the Question of Compensation

This document was prepared by Bozell, Jacobs, Kenyon and Eckhardt as an internal report. We reprint it with permission. (Bozell is now part of True North Communications Inc.)

I. Introduction: The BJK&E Point of View

Over the past several years, in an environment in which increasingly varied and complex agency/client compensation arrangements are more the norm than the exception, a great deal of attention has been focused on so-called performance-based compensation agreements. (The term *performance-based compensation* shall, for the purposes of this discussion, refer to agency remuneration systems that include any of the following elements, alone or in combination: performance reviews, incentives, or bonuses.)

Before getting into the details of performance-based compensation, it is important to make BJK&E's point of view clear at the outset: We enthusiastically endorse the trend toward performance-based compensation arrangements. BJK&E is eager to explore, with current and prospective clients, the benefits of mutually shared risks and rewards. Because of its "Close to the Customer" ethos and its commitment to true marketing partnerships, BJK&E must seek every opportunity to enhance agency revenues by contributing to client successes.

Despite their growing popularity, translating the *concept* of performance-based systems into the *reality* of a mutually beneficial financial relationship can present an agency with serious problems. For instance, when an agency has served its client satisfactorily under a commission or fee arrangement, the agency may have difficulty facing a situation in which it must meet new (and sometimes vague) standards of performance or achievement. Perhaps even more daunting, the agency may be asked to accept a revenue base that, before incentives, is projected at a level substantially below existing guaranteed income.

The issue is not a simple one, nor is there a surefire, one-size-fits-all answer. For agency and client to maintain a healthy and productive relationship, the right answers should emerge from a journey of discovery. The journey must be based on mutual trust. Anything less is hopeless.

The road map must reflect agreement on equitable compensation criteria that serve client needs, agency needs, and shared needs.

Most significantly, compensation must be treated as an integrated issue, inseparable from the quality of the agency's work, the quantity of the agency's workload, the staffing requirements, the particular nature and demands of the brand or brands, and the history of the relationship. (Obviously, compensation matters can arise at any time. Ideally, they should be discussed in the course of regular agency performance reviews. Then the focus is macro, positive, and constructive, rather than isolated on financial-only issues.)

II. The Scope of This Document

This document is intended to provide an up-to-date review of the issue of performance-based compensation so that BJK&E executives who are involved in negotiating agency/client commissions and fees understand the advantages and risks in this relatively new area.

The sections that follow include a review of overall compensation trends; the benefits and pitfalls of performance-based systems, an investigation of some of the motives that drive clients to explore performance-based options, a look at several of the agency/client agreements that have been published in trade magazines, a discussion of other known variations, and, finally, an outline of the four basic principles that should guide BJK&E executives in compensation negotiations involving potential performance-based agreements.

III. Context: Recent Trends in Agency Compensation

The Association of National Advertisers (ANA), representing the largest client companies in the United States, has regularly analyzed compensation trends in the advertising industry and published its findings. The survey results have been relatively consistent for the past decade, as reflected in these highlights from the most recent (1995) study:

The traditional 15 percent commission system, the dominant form of agency remuneration through the mid- to late eighties, continues to decline in popularity. Today, among ANA members, the 15 percent commission remains the province of only a few of the very largest advertisers (P&G, Kellogg, General Mills, and General Electric, among them). Full 15 percent commission arrangements now account for only 14 percent of the reported relationships. (Irony: Many small, non-ANA advertisers, recognizing that cost-based systems would require higher fees, continue to prefer 15 percent commissions.)

Sliding-scale commission systems, typically starting at or near 15 percent and using a declining commission rate for incremental spending above a base budget, grew in popularity for about ten years. The use of this compensation option has now stabilized at 21 percent of reporting companies.

Flat commissions below 15 percent continue to grow in use among major client companies. Of the advertisers in the ANA survey, 24 percent now report reduced commissions as a primary compensation system. This compensation alternative retains many of the advantages of the historical commission system—simplicity, projectability, ease of administration—yet it eliminates client concerns about unreasonable or excess agency profits.

Cost-based fee systems now account for the largest share of agency/client relationships among ANA members, with 45 percent of the companies reporting use of one or more types of fee arrangements. The increased popularity of cost-based systems—now widely endorsed by both advertisers and agencies—is where approaches to performance incentives have made the most obvious inroads.

IV. Performance-Based Compensation: Benefits and Pitfalls

The growing interest in performance-based compensation is easily understandable, as both clients and agencies embrace the concept of accountability in many aspects of their businesses.

At least in theory, the advantages of these incentive systems seem conclusive on first glance. They focus the agency (and the advertiser) on the client's key objectives. They create a healthy and mutually supportive dialogue on a number of important issues, ranging from the validity of the stated objectives, to the marketplace priorities, to the evaluation of results. And they offer the promise of shared rewards (earned benefits, not windfalls) for outstanding accomplishments.

Unfortunately, the potential disadvantages of performance-based systems often turn the translation from theory to practice into a daunting task—or, at the very least, a challenging one. Incentive systems create the possibility of increased compensation costs for the client. They may also result in reduced base compensation for the agency. In either event, projecting actual costs and/or revenue becomes more difficult for both parties, and stable projections are often not possible until the end of the client's fiscal year.

In an environment in which virtually all cost-based compensation systems have burdened both clients and agencies with increased administrative responsibilities, performance-based systems add significant complexity to the oversight tasks and inevitably result in greater time and cost allocations.

Evaluative criteria can become too complex or too subjective as negotiators attempt to foresee every eventuality or reduce complex relationships to neat mathematical equations. Sometimes the result is a theoretical incentive that becomes an actual disincentive—which occurs when a seemingly reasonable goal becomes clearly unattainable in a volatile marketplace.

Finally, evaluations may ignore or paper over problems on the client side—problems that inhibit the agency's ability to perform up to the stated objectives.

Evaluation criteria for the agency are often different than those for client personnel (as they should be). However, problems may arise when a client company has a good year, exceeds objectives, and significantly rewards its marketing executives. If, for whatever reasons, there is no bonus for the agency, relations may become strained. (When the opposite is true—when the agency receives an incentive payment and the client doesn't—the risks are even more likely to damage an otherwise healthy working relationship.)

V. Motivation: What Drives Client Interest in Performance-Based Compensation Arrangements?

The ability of BKJ&E agencies to respond cooperatively to a client request for consideration of a performance-based compensation system will, in large measure, be determined by the reasonableness of the request and the primary motivation behind it.

While there are a number of reasons that may stimulate a client's interest in exploring a new compensation arrangement, three are most common:

1. Alignment with Other Purchasing Systems

Clients, having made major changes in the way they purchase goods and services, may be motivated by a desire to bring agency compensation into line with incentive-based programs already instituted in other areas of their business. During the 1980s and early 1990s, many companies substituted new reward-oriented programs for the ones traditionally in place in cost categories as diverse as employee compensation and vendor purchasing. These substitutions were intended to provide greater motivation to the affected parties, reduce fixed committed costs where possible, meet new shareholder standards, and generally apply a new philosophy to the company's operations—a philosophy that would ultimately build shareholder value.

When clients with this type of motivation approach their agencies to discuss compensation, the resulting program may well provide mutual benefits. More to the point, if the client has had success with similar arrangements, it will be difficult and probably unwise for the agency to offer strong resistance. The request reflects an evolving client culture, and there is at least a reasonable potential for bringing about changes that will result in a strengthened relationship.

2. Exploration of a Popular Current Trend

A second common motivation for raising the issue of performance-based agency compensation is the desire to improve the existing agreement by gaining experience with a popular, if somewhat elusive, new idea. Some companies may have been exposed to the concept of incentive compensation programs through stories in the trade press or other publications, or at industry meetings. Others may have had their interest heightened by new employees who had experience with similar systems at other companies. Still others may be attracted to performance-based systems as a result of their ongoing discomfort with the effectiveness of their compensation arrangements. Finally, outside consultants have played an increasingly important role in stimulating experimentation with new compensation programs.

Under any of these circumstances, if the agency acknowledges the existence of serious problems in the current compensation system, then the client's motive for exploring alternatives is acceptable. If, however, the agency's work is outstanding and the agency is being fairly remunerated, it may well be appropriate to resist the idea of change for the sake of change. Just because an untested idea is new and seemingly logical, it does not necessarily follow that equitable existing systems should be dismantled or that a new system will bring about improvements, operational or financial.

3. Fee Reduction Without Regard for Agency Costs

We believe that some clients and prospective clients are motivated simply by the drive to reduce expenses—without any real consideration of the agency's cost structure for servicing the business. Ultimately, this kind of attitude will destroy an agency/client bond. In the short term, it must be actively resisted in hopes of eventually placing the relationship on stronger footing.

In facing this kind of situation—whether or not it involves an outside compensation consultant—the agency will operate at a significant negotiating disadvantage if it cannot associate real costs with the services provided. Moreover, the agency executives involved in compensation discussions must understand (and be able to explain) their own cost accounting systems—and must be confident that the data provided to the client or consultants are accurate and fully auditable.

Reductions in client compensation expenses without compensating agency cost reductions represent a clearly unacceptable basis for renegotiating agency/client fees, even when the potential for incentive compensation is offered. Therefore, if sheer cost reduction is judged to be the dominant motive, it must be recognized as such, and the agency must bring to bear its most significant resources. Finding an equitable resolution may be impossible when only one party cares about equity. Common ground is even harder to find if the client company is driven solely by a desire to deliver the largest possible cost reduction regardless of its impact on the underlying relationship.

Clearly, the most critical issue BJK&E executives face in evaluating requests for compensation renegotiation is judging the basic client motive. If we understand the motive at the start of discussions, there is a more than reasonable likelihood of finding a solution with long-term benefits. Misjudging the motives presents immediate peril for the agency.

VI. The Published Performance-Based Systems

The performance-based compensation systems summarized on the following page have been exposed to the public through *Advertising Age*, *Adweek*, and other industry publications:

Client	Agency	System Description
AT&T	FCB/Leber Katz Young & Rubicam Ayer McCann Erickson BBD&O	Cost-plus fee plus bonuses based upon meeting objectives
Blimpie	Kirschenbaurn & Bond	Fee plus stock option on Blimpie stock (used with other Kirschenbaurn & Bond clients as well)
Colgate	FCB/Leber Katz Y&R	Commission at rate below 15% plus bonus based on brand sales results
Kraft, General Foods	Burnett J. Walter Thompson Young & Rubicam Ogilvy & Mather Grey Agency Foote Cone Belding	Commission based on 13–14% plus incentives based on predetermined goals, such as brand sales and evaluation of agency
Mazda	Foote Cone Belding	Total compensation based on number of cars the client sells
Saturn	Hal Riney & Partners	Base fee plus sliding-scale incentive program based on sales, awareness of ads, and ability to generate first-time purchases
Starbucks, Pepsi J.V.	Hal Riney	Base fee plus incentives based on sales, awareness, and consumer take-away impressions.

VII. Other Performance-Based Agreements

1. Commission Plus Bonus Linked to Objectives

Another type of performance-based agreement uses a sliding-scale commission system, plus agreement on agency objectives, which are reviewed throughout the year and then graded at year-end. (Grades are outstanding, very good, average, or poor.) Bonuses are computed, using agreed-upon objective weights, as a percentage of commissions paid:

- 20 percent for outstanding grade
- 10 percent for very good grade
- 0 percent for grading of average or poor

2. Base Plus Markup Plus Bonus

An alternative is a cost-based fee plus a 10 percent profit markup. In addition, evaluation of the agency's performance at year-end by the client can yield a bonus of up to 15 percent (on the fee plus profit). Therefore, at maximum level, this system would yield a profit margin of 20.9 percent as calculated below:

Base	Markup	Profit
100	10%	10.0
110	15%	16.5
Total		26.5

A profit of 26.5 on total cost plus profit of 126.5 yields a profit margin of 20.9 percent.

3. Fee Plus Markup Based on Focus Group Score

Agencies receive a cost-based fee with no profit. Profit can then range from a 0 percent to 30 percent markup, based on the scores derived from focus groups organized by a mutually agreed-upon outside research source.

VIII. How to Proceed: Four Principles

BJK&E executives face inherent challenges whenever a current client or prospect approaches the agency with a request to convert an existing compensation program to an incentive, performance-based system. However, since the client may have perfectly valid reasons for the request, the agency must not assume that total resistance is the appropriate response. Instead, we should adhere to four overarching principles when addressing the issue of incentive compensation.

1. Understand the Client Culture

The underlying culture of the client company—and the fundamental nature of the client's business—will often substantially influence the level of interest in exploring incentive compensation options. Therefore, to assure a cooperative approach to the issue, and an equitable resolution, BJK&E executives must focus sharply on what drives client behavior. For instance:

- A retail-oriented client with an emphasis on short-term, measurable sales results may prefer very quantitative evaluative criteria, while a client running a corporate image campaign may lean toward more qualitative evaluation.
- An advertiser who is preoccupied with the price of its company stock will probably want to tie compensation, in some form, to market performance, while a creatively driven client is more likely to build copy test scores into the equation.
- A client with a mature brand in a stable category may concentrate on advertising effectiveness, measured by share growth, while a company with a new product entry may want to track initial trial and repurchase.
- A company in a highly cyclical industry may want to limit base agency profits in lean years, while offering higher upside opportunities in good times.

Rarely, of course, does a client's business and culture fit simply and neatly into these categories. So it will take long, hard, creative thinking to find common ground. (And remember what H. L. Mencken wrote: "For every problem, there is one solution which is simple, neat and wrong.")

2. Assure an Acceptable Level of Minimum Compensation

Base compensation should be sufficient to cover agency costs, including direct salaries and reasonable employee bonuses, overhead, direct expenses, and a minimum profit (not less than 10 percent). The agency cannot be expected to put all of its profits at risk, since profits are required to fund capital expenses and shareholder return. It is especially unfair to eliminate all profit from the base compensation in fee and incentive arrangements because, by their very nature, negotiated compensation systems—with or without incentives—place a limit on the agency's potential profitability.

It is interesting to note that Alvin Achenbaum, then heading Canter, Achenbaum Associates, the most important client consultant in the compensation area, said in the late eighties, "Incentive compensation provides a means of offering larger profits for those agencies that do a better job and *ordinary profits for those agencies that perform up to snuff.*" (Italics added to indicate that even the clients' counselors did not intend for agencies to put all of their profits at risk.)

3. Work Toward Measurable Standards of Achievement

It will inevitably prove unwise to accept performance evaluation standards that are based entirely on a client's subjective judgments. While it is impossible to eliminate subjectivity in all cases, BJK&E executives should aim to strike a balance between objective measures and subjective standards. Otherwise, there is a risk of too strong a value placed on the views of one client executive (not to mention the risk of client personnel changes during the year). Similarly, there is always the threat of an agency's potential incentive payments being used to cover a client's budget shortfall.

No standards are perfect. But simple, straightforward, objective standards are better than none at all. One possibility, for instance, might be to index the agency bonus structure to the percentage of salary bonus awarded to the client's senior marketing executives.

4. Include the Potential for Significantly Enhanced Profits

It is unacceptable to consider incentive compensation programs that provide a maximum profit potential no higher than the profit range that has been traditional in nonincentive agency/client agreements. Normal business practice dictates that greater risks must be accompanied by the opportunity for greater rewards.

Most advertising industry authorities (the ANA, the American Association of Advertising Agencies, and outside consultants) have, for many years, generally agreed that an agency profit goal of 15 percent to 20 percent on revenues is equitable. It follows, therefore, that the profit included in the base fee plus the maximum profit achievable under an incentive system should yield a performance-based total profit of at least 25 percent—preferably in the 30 percent range. (This meets the first element of Achenbaum's view, offering larger profits for those agencies that do a better job.)

Based on the four principles previously described, the model for an equitable performance-based compensation plan would include these basic elements:

- A base fee equal to the estimated costs for servicing the account (labor plus benefits, including a reasonable employee bonus, plus overhead)
- A profit of at least 10 percent added to the base fee
- Out-of-pocket costs incurred in—and directly related to—servicing the account, added to the fee
- An incentive schedule ranging up to 20 percent of the base fee plus fee profit, paid annually, and calculated on the basis of measurable objectives and a subjective performance review

These issues are extremely important. Please feel free to consult with BJK&E corporate management whenever dealing with a performance-based system.

Interest in incentive programs is unlikely to disappear in the near future. In fact, these concepts may achieve even greater penetration of agency/client compensation agreements. At the very least, they will be on the table for discussion. Therefore, BJK&E executives need to understand the risks and opportunities and become proactive in response to client initiatives.

In the end, regardless of the nature of the compensation plan, it must deliver value to both the client and the agency. That is the surest way to continue to grow our clients' businesses and our own.

Index